PRACTI
SOCIAL V

Series Editor: Jo Campling

Social work is at an important stage in its development. All professions must be responsive to changing social and economic conditions if they are to meet the needs of those they serve. This series focuses on sound practice and the specific contributions which social workers can make to the well-being of our society.

The British Association of Social Workers has always been conscious of its role in setting guidelines for practice and in seeking to raise professional standards. The conception of the Practical Social Work series arose from a survey of BASW members to discover where they, the practitioners in social work, felt there was the most need for new literature. The response was overwhelming and enthusiastic, and the result is a carefully planned, coherent series of books. The emphasis is firmly on practice set in a theoretical framework. The books will inform, stimulate and promote discussion, thus adding to the further development of skills and high professional standards. All the authors are practitioners and teachers of social work, representing a wide variety of experience.

JO CAMPLING

A list of published titles in this series follows overleaf

Practical Social Work
Series Standing Order ISBN 0–333–69347–7
(*outside North America only*)

You can receive future titles in this series as they are published by placing a standing order. Please contact your bookseller or, in the case of difficulty, write to us at the address below with your name and address, the title of the series and the ISBN quoted above.

Customer Services Department, Macmillan Distribution Ltd
Houndmills, Basingstoke, Hampshire RG21 6XS, England

PRACTICAL SOCIAL WORK

Series Editor: Jo Campling

BASW

For Sue and Barbara,
Robin, Isobel, Juliet, Jamie, Barnaby

Contents

Introduction

The seeds of this book were sown in the early 1980s when we were both working at the National Institute for Social Work. Community work as a purposeful process of working with or for communities had existed in rural areas to a limited extent since the 1920s but the late 1970s saw a more rapid growth.

We were aware, however, that expansion in rural community work practice had not been matched by thinking or writing about the principles which lay behind the practice. There had been an increasing understanding about a wide range of rural problems (housing, service provision, agricultural change, etc.) and about policies and solutions, and people were calling for greater community involvement in addressing these issues. Yet, with very few exceptions, there had been little attention given to the 'how and why' of rural community work in any depth.

It was not until the late 1980s, when we met again in the North of England, that the book began to take shape. It soon became apparent that a manual of community work skills and methods would not be enough. Rural community work, in its various forms, is a practice which is conditioned by the geography of rural areas, the social structure and culture of villages and small country towns, the values prevalent in community groups and agencies, traditions, and the resources which are available. In order to make choices about what to do and how to do it, it is necessary to understand those factors which condition rural community work practice, and we have therefore included appropriate material about this context. A key feature of this book is that it brings together ideas and information about community development and other types of intervention, much of which has been drawn from situations which are urban, with material about issues, communities and agencies which is specifically rural.

Geographically, we have drawn on material from all parts of the UK and, to a lesser extent, from mainland Europe and further afield. We have not confined ourselves to any particular sort of agency or discipline. In our travels, we spoke to social workers, youth workers, adult education workers, clergy and planners, as well as community workers – both paid and voluntary. The fact that community work focuses on people means that the appearance of this book in a practical social work series has a special relevance but we would not argue that social work is necessarily of greater significance than any other avenue into the practice of rural community work.

Community work is a process of helping groups in the community to develop, in order to tackle their needs, disadvantage or inequality. Community work helps people to identify their needs, to come together in a group, to be supported in the action which they decide to take in order to achieve their goals. It is a learning process, encouraging people collectively to improve their skills, confidence, awareness and understanding, in order to acquire resources and influence. Often, the issues may span a number of different fields, such as health, social services, education, housing, employment, the environment, recreation, the arts. Community work is also concerned with making the services of statutory, voluntary and private organisations more flexible, relevant and responsive to people's needs and demands.

Many of the features of rural community work practice are common to all sorts of environment, but there are also some significant differences which contrast with the classic community work model which has emerged from neighbourhood work in inner city and peripheral urban estate settings. The classic model depends upon proximity, contact and access, both between members of the community, and between the community and the community worker. This model emphasises that the community worker has to spend a great deal of time within the neighbourhood which he or she serves: gaining the trust of local people, being available, and being on the spot to help individuals and groups through the processes of development and problem-solving. However, this degree of availability is rarely possible in rural areas.

Assumptions of planners and policy-makers about the concentration of needs and problems do not hold good in rural areas. Rural neighbourhoods are rarely so homogeneous, and those individuals who are deprived may well be hidden: either as a result of physical isolation, or by their own reluctance to let their neighbours see that they have problems, or by the actions of better-off residents in the same neighbourhood working to gloss over, or even suppress, local expressions of need or deprivation.

Community work is as dependent as any other 'social intervention' on the availability of human resources, and in rural areas these rarely match up to what might be expected in urban areas. Because of these factors, the reality of rural community work is that most workers have no alternative but to cover a wide geographical area. Possibilities for adopting a neighbourhood-based approach are far from being the norm in rural areas.

Faced with these opportunities and limitations, rural community work has evolved appropriate strategies and a set of tools to cope. They include the skills and techniques of supporting groups at arm's length: via the telephone, correspondence, newsletters, irregular face-to-face contact. Methods are used to penetrate the surface gloss of rural communities, to reach those in need and help them find effective solutions. Special ways are developed for working with the small or scattered communities of many rural areas, where the incidence of common problems and of people able and willing to take action is often low. So, too, are techniques for the workers to take the initiative.

At the heart of this book is a model of rural community work practice. This is explained in Chapter 4, and in the following three chapters we examine its various elements in more detail. These are set in the context of the geography and social and political structures of rural areas, the agencies involved, the resources available and the ethos of rural development. The book will be of interest to community workers and community work students and also those in related fields, such as clergy, volunteer organisers, social workers, youth workers, adult educationists, environmentalists, primary health care teams, etc. It is also of relevance to those who control the resources for rural community work at local and national level, and those involved in other aspects of rural development who may be interested to learn more about the significance of community-based action to their work.

The book is applicable to community work in a variety of settings. Rural areas and communities differ widely, from the apparently wealthy commuter villages which are close to most towns and cities, through to the remote, marginal and often poorer upland areas. We have tried to take account of the less common situations – the old mining communities, new villages, urban estates in the countryside – as well as classic farming or fishing villages. Inevitably we make generalisations, but every community *is* different, and no community worker should try to rely on a textbook as a substitute for what they should learn from first-hand experience of direct observation and interaction.

Acknowledgements

We have been greatly helped by a small advisory panel, who have made invaluable contributions both directly to the content of the book and by giving us useful leads to follow up. Members of the panel included Ann Meadows, from ACRE (Action with Communities in Rural England); Avila Kilmurray, formerly of the Northern Ireland Rural Action Project; Rory MacLeod from Borders Regional Council, Scotland; Alan Rogers from Wye College, University of London; David Thomas, from the Community Development Foundation (CDF); and Arthur Davies, formerly of the Wales Association of County Voluntary Councils.

We have also been given special help by two national organisations. CDF provided the secretariat for the project and ACRE gave encouragement and practical help, and made available their library. Kevin Harris, CDF's Information Officer, also chased up books and articles, and Ann Nicholls at CDF's Leeds office provided welcome administrative support. Above all, Elisabeth Haarhaus of Leeds did sterling work on her wordprocessor. Her efficiency and patience during the re-drafting period were particularly appreciated.

The inspiration and examples for the book have come directly from practitioners throughout the United Kingdom. In 1989, we held a skills exchange workshop which drew in specially invited, experienced rural community workers from a variety of agencies and settings. During that same year, we travelled extensively to visit local community work projects and agencies, which greatly enhanced our appreciation of life at the sharp end, as well as telling us more about the issues involved.

During the preparation and writing of this book we became increasingly aware of the variety of rural practitioners with whom we were in contact, and of the amount of detailed material about practice we had accumulated. Accordingly, a collection of case studies -*Rural Action – A Collection of Community Work Case Studies* (Henderson and Francis 1992) was produced. We are very pleased that such a practice volume grew out of our contact with rural community workers.

We had the privilege, and benefit, of having our research and writing generously supported. We are extremely grateful to the following organisations: the Calouste Gulbenkian Foundation, the Joseph Rowntree Charitable Trust, the Chase Charity, the Charities Aid Foundation, Marks & Spencer plc, Royal Bank of Scotland plc, Barclays Bank plc and National Westminster Bank plc.

Finally, we acknowledge with thanks the guidance and support given by Jo Campling, and her colleagues at the publishers. They kept us going at the end of a long, enjoyable project.

DAVID FRANCIS
PAUL HENDERSON

1

Rural Development and Community Work

The latter half of the twentieth century has confronted people in rural areas with an almost unprecedented scale and pace of change. From the accessible commuter villages close to our larger cities to the remotest parts of the United Kingdom, many of the traditional features of rural life are being eroded and frequently replaced by unfamiliar and threatening signs. Farming is a dwindling source of employment and wealth in many areas. Young people are leaving their home areas, pushed out by increasingly unaffordable housing, and attracted away by better job and leisure prospects. The proportion of older people is growing and traditional patterns of family and neighbourly care have largely disappeared. Furthermore, the forces of change are increasingly coming from distant places, beyond the immediate grasp of local people.

Faced with these changes, a traditional response from many rural people is to do nothing but reluctantly and individually to accept them. Yet that is an increasingly untenable and difficult position. There is a growing realisation that people need to organise themselves within their communities and localities, to take action to improve their collective lot. Community-based action is not a new idea, but it is of growing relevance in a society which views the maintenance of many small rural communities as economically unviable, and which is content to keep them marginalised to the further disadvantage of those who are already the weakest in society.

Community-based action, whether it is a self-help or a campaigning affair, can happen spontaneously, but to be effective it frequently requires something extra: the right information and

1

advice; a little encouragement when spirits are flagging; an injection of grant aid; a wider perspective on a local problem.

Community development is about 'getting things done' – building a children's play area, saving a school from closure, caring for people with a disability – but it is also about the creative development of people – people working together to support each other, involving and giving power and responsibility to disadvantaged people, growing in confidence and competence through active participation, confronting inequalities in society. Community development can be supported by a number of professionals, not just community workers.

Community work is a form of 'intervention' which enables local people to reap maximum benefit from community-based action and community development. It is an action-based set of values, methods, skills and techniques.

Local action and community development

A number of benefits can come from community development, which can broadly be typified as functional and developmental purposes.

Functional purposes:

———   An active and mutually supportive community can organise and deliver services, jobs, environmental improvements etc. which are no longer seen as viable within the public and private sectors. Examples include co-operatively organised shops, voluntary minibus services, neighbourhood care schemes. In rural areas these may be not so much alternatives to conventional state or commercial provision, but the only available options.

———   Motivated and organised communities can take action to combat the decline in services, jobs and the environment through strategies such as lobbying, protest, persuasion and encouragement, in a variety of possible relationships with the agencies or bodies which take or influence decisions. Examples include campaigns against school closures, surveys and negotiations to improve local bus services, 'use it or lose it' campaigns which encourage local residents to patronise the local post office more fully.

Developmental purposes:

—— Participation in community-based action enables people to grow in confidence and competence, collectively giving them and their communities self-respect and greater influence and control over their future. For example, participation in a pre-school playgroup management committee will present many young parents (mainly women) with a chance to discuss wider common problems, to learn about the system and policies which affect the lives of themselves and their children, and begin to diversify into, for example, mutual family support, lobbying for better childcare provision or helping to run the local village hall.

—— Taking action as part of a community not only strengthens and affirms the community as the key local social system within which people interact, it also develops the skill, awareness and outlook of the individual for understanding and participating in wider social and political processes. Democracy in society is highly dependent upon social interaction and development at a local community level.

Effective community work practice requires the functional and developmental purposes of community development to be kept in balance. Over-emphasis on outcome or product would deprive community work of the dimension of human change and the idea of process. Conversely, to be concerned only with process, at the expense of achieving tangible results, would also be a distortion of community work. Keeping this balance is as important for social workers, clergy, youth workers and others who are essentially using community work as a method as it is for community workers.

Not everything that rural agencies and their staff do in communities can be classified as community work. This definitional point can be illustrated by village hall work:

A community worker. A community worker might identify an opportunity to work with a village hall committee. The aim would be to use this forum to develop people's skills in relating to each other, identifying external resources and power and learning more about the needs of people in the community. In the process better village hall provision would come about.

A specialist utilising a community work method. Village halls specialists want to see effective village halls because they believe they make a valuable contribution to village life. However, in order to achieve effective village halls they recognise that a wide cross-section of people need to be involved, people need to learn to work together. They therefore use a community work method for part of their time whilst at other times they may be gathering and providing specialist advice about hall maintenance, lobbying central government etc. in order to get a better deal for village halls in general. These latter activities in themselves are not community work (Ann Meadows, personal communication, 1990).

Community-based action involves a number of components, which are in many cases choices or alternatives and, at times, may actually be in conflict. Hugh Butcher *et al.* (1980) identify these choices under three headings:

(1) *The motives underlying action by individuals in community groups.* These motives include: mutual aid ('by undertaking to help one another, all may help themselves' – Beveridge, 1948); philanthropy (helping one's fellows, from a social conscience); and sociability (a desire to meet people and make friends).
(2) *The material objective of the community group's strategy.* These objectives include: influence (i.e. negotiation, joint planning, lobbying); and service-provision (e.g. community-run playgroups, businesses, village halls).
(3) *The nature of the social relationships.* Relationships within society may be seen as: consensus (i.e. common interest, values and purpose); co-operation (i.e. willingness of differing groups to work together); or conflict.

It would be wrong to see all community-based action as *inherently* a 'good thing'. The sorts of choices which Butcher *et al.* outline above have to be put into a wider context – the action which community groups take has to be seen in relation to wider political processes.

The local–national debate

For many years, community development has been challenged by a major argument, known to many practitioners as the 'CDP Analysis' because of its association with many of the Home Office-sponsored Community Development Projects of the early

1970s. The argument is that the fundamental causes of social inequality are structural, rooted within society at a national and not merely local level. Solutions must therefore be at a national level, which will almost inevitably mean a strategy of conflict and struggle, and any action taken by communities locally to help themselves will, at best, be superficial but more seriously may be a dangerous deflection from tackling the real causes.

In his study of poverty in Britain, Townsend (1979) echoes this argument:

> Areas or communities cannot be treated as autonomous or self-sufficient in terms either of autonomy or culture...The pattern of inequality within them is set nationally...It is the national structure of unequal resource allocation, especially in its outcomes for classes and social minorities on the one hand, and the sponsorship of styles of living and modes of consumption by powerful market state institutions on the other, which primarily explains area deprivation.

For some community workers, one of the outcomes of this analysis was a mistrust and rejection of local community-based action. In his commentary on rural policy in the 1980s, McLaughlin (1987) took a similar, but not quite so dismissive, stance in questioning an over-dependence by the state (as evidenced by such agencies as the Rural Development Commission) on a philosophy of rural self-help at an individual and community level. He rightly pointed out that romantic images of the rural idyll and of local approaches can be a smokescreen to hide serious structural problems within rural society, and to direct attention away from state intervention on a variety of fronts at a national level.

However, taking a more pluralistic line, Alan Rogers (1987) has argued that it would be wrong to undervalue local community action as a crucial aspect of rural development. Problems affecting people in rural areas have a multiplicity of causes, some deep-rooted in the structure of society and some derived more locally, and action should be taken to ameliorate the effects of problems, as well as trying to tackle their root causes.

The rural context

Well-grounded, community-based action must stem from a community's own identification and interpretation of problems, needs and opportunities, and from its own choice of appropriate action. However, there is a wealth of published material which people in rural areas, as well as community workers and policy-makers, can draw upon to put their situation into a wider context. It is important that they do so, for several reasons:

(i)   If community work is to help people to adopt a critical perspective towards the problems which they identify, then a broad and deep understanding of rural problems is needed; broad, in order to see local problems in the wider context of social, economic, political and physical change affecting the locality, society and the world at large; deep, in order to see people's current perception of problems in the historical context of a local social system which has developed over time, and which will continue to evolve in the future.

(ii) Some of the 'wider' problems may not yet be obvious, or may not yet have impinged on the locality, and so a broader understanding of the trends can alert people. It can help the community to anticipate change, not just react to it retrospectively.

(iii) While there is no substitute for direct experience, many community workers, policy-makers, professionals and residents are new to the rural scene and familiarisation with existing knowledge about 'rural problems' should be an important part of their induction.

Since the 1970s, there has been a significant increase in the literature about rural areas and rural issues, largely as the result of a growth of interest by policy-makers, academics and professionals. We can give only an outline of the literature in the following pages.

'Rural issues' include two overlapping components:

——   the broad trends affecting rural areas (e.g. changes in agriculture, the dilution of rural culture)
——   problems affecting people in rural areas, which may have much in common with problems in urban situations (e.g. unemployment, poor housing)

Rural trends

Rural areas are not homogeneous, and the issues affecting different localities, and different people within them, can be very varied (see

Champion and Watkins, 1991). Nevertheless, it is possible to identify some broad trends which are familiar not only in most rural parts of the United Kingdom, but also in the rest of Western Europe:

(i) *Selective population shifts between town and country.* Agriculture and other primary industries began to shed labour in the nineteenth century, resulting in a drift from the land into towns and cities, a process which continues today albeit not on such a large scale. In the more accessible countryside closer to the urban areas, there is a movement in the opposite direction as urban people (typified in an over-generalised way as wealthy, middle-class professionals and retired people) move to the villages and country towns which have acquired a higher social status. This effect, which has been labelled 'counter-urbanisation', is a complex combination of forces and processes. Demographically, the rural population may be static or even growing, but sociologically there are enormous changes as the local, predominantly working-class rural people are eclipsed or displaced by urban people of quite different class, background and values. The high level of personal mobility for many of these incomers means that these trends are identifiable even in villages which in the mid-twentieth century were seen as 'remote and unchanged'.

There is still a decline in population in the remoter areas, but even here the out-migration (or lack of natural increase) by local people is to some extent countered by an influx of retired people, the tourism and leisure industry, and people seeking an 'alternative rural lifestyle'. Arguably, it is no longer possible to identify a locality or community in any rural part of the United Kingdom which bears a close resemblance to a 'traditional rural community'.

The population shifts and adjustments have implications for those rural people who are displaced, for those who stay, and for those who move into rural areas. There are gainers and losers in the interplay between these different interests: a point which we come back to in our next chapter on the nature of rural communities.

(ii) *Changing employment structure.* The shedding of labour by agriculture, fishing, forestry, quarrying and coal-mining seems likely to continue into the twenty-first century, partly as a consequence of increased mechanisation, but also due to changing world markets, government policy and public attitudes. There has been some success in attracting new work in manufacturing and services, some of it by reorientating and diversifying local businesses, and some by moving industries out from the urban areas. The late twentieth century has seen many lowland rural areas attracting footloose high-technology industries (such as computer programming and laser engineering) which put more value on having an attractive rural environment for their staff than on being readily accessible to urban markets.

However, in many rural areas the wage rates are low, the skills of local people are not directly relevant to those which employers need, much of the work is seasonal (especially tourism and agriculture), unemployment and under-employment are still unacceptably high, and the local economy is vulnerable due to the dominance by a large employer whose decisions on employment matters are taken by a head office outside the area. Despite these problems, there is frequently a fear of new employers moving into the area, with activities which are unacceptable environmentally (e.g. a nuclear waste reprocessing plant) or socially (e.g. an abattoir), which has resulted in a widespread resistance to new industrial and employment development. It is a considerable challenge to find for rural areas a diverse range of enterprises which are not too vulnerable to factors outside local control, which are acceptable to local residents and which are based to a large extent on local skills and enterprise.

(iii) *Decline of services.* Most rural areas have experienced a decline of public and private sector services since the 1950s and 1960s. Various factors have been significant: population decline; the increased use of private transport to use services in nearby towns; the increasing unit-cost of servicing a small, scattered rural population; the increased efficiency and quality which specialised, centralised services seem to offer; a lack of sensitivity by service providers to the needs of rural areas. Since the 1970s, the inevitability of some of these processes has been challenged by pressure groups and local communities, with some success in, for example, retaining a primary school which had been scheduled for closure, or securing improvements to the local telephone system.

The decline of rural services has not affected all people in a locality equally. It has hit hardest those who have been most dependent on the service, and who do not have easy access to an alternative: the elderly, teenagers, disabled people, young isolated women. The decline has also affected the vitality and viability of communities as a whole, particularly when key services, such as the only public meeting-place (e.g. a school or pub), are lost.

(iv) *Less sympathetic political climate.* Since the mid-1970s, there have been cutbacks by the UK government in the resources available and (more recently) in the role which the public sector can play in meeting people's needs. Part of the effect of this has been to precipitate the decline in public services outlined above, but another impact of the more competitive, market-orientated style of the 1990s has been to marginalise still further those areas and groups which have not been well placed to 'work the system'. The imposition of competitive tendering for contracts, of efficiency-orientated policies, of performance-related payment to public service providers, and the removal of barriers to trade, all work in favour of accessible and concentrated 'markets' and against those areas and people which are disadvantaged by their geography, and which do not have a culture which accords with the spirit of individual competition.

(v) *Erosion of culture.* Population movements and the introduction of powerful outside influences through television, education and advertising, have brought about a marked erosion of local rural cultures, and a challenge to long-held and deeply-rooted values. Especially in Scotland, Wales and Ireland, the survival of the traditional language has also been undermined. Cultural change and conflict is often aligned with other conflicts, based upon social class, wealth, status differences and values, but the relationships are usually more complex. Calls to preserve 'the rural way of life' can be used to improve or to exacerbate the conditions of disadvantaged people, and should be treated cautiously. Added to this complexity is the growing difficulty in many parts of the UK, especially in England, of pinpointing just what the local rural culture actually is, and in deciding what should be the activities and outcomes of community-based action, based upon the idea of 'local culture'.

(vi) *Growing divides.* The greater mixture of people in rural communities than before has not been accompanied by any degree of increased social equality between people. It is difficult to plot these changes over time, but indicators such as persistently low agricultural wages, the prohibitively high market values of owner-occupied housing, and the materially impoverished lifestyles of many elderly people in rural areas, seem to suggest that the contrast between the 'haves' and 'have-nots' is, if anything, becoming wider than ever. The wealth of the better-off does not rub off on to people in poverty, simply through living side-by-side. Ironically, there is a widely held perception, from outside the rural areas, that such areas are generally well-off. The existence of some very wealthy people, taken in combination with attractive rural environments and overall a slower and apparently less conflictive and competitive way-of-life, all too often lead to an understandable but erroneous perception of the countryside as a place of harmony and content-ment.

(vii) *Declining public resources.* Most rural local authorities are conservative in outlook, and tend to spend less per capita on services than their urban equivalents (Cloke, 1988). In recent years, cutbacks in government subsidies for local services, and the increasing cost of provision, have led to an inevitable belt-tight-ening. These reductions have hit hardest at the margins: the remoter rural localities, the innovative services which focus on special needs, and on types of work which are seen as being outside the main-stream. Rural areas – and community development and area-wide voluntary organisations within them – have been particularly badly hit by this retrenchment.

(viii) *Increasing environmental awareness.* Since the late 1960s there has been a growing awareness of the need to retain and enhance the quality of the environment. Conflicts have arisen through economic development pressures (road-building, out-of-town retailing, mineral extraction, intensive agriculture, forestry) and growing demands for recreation in the countryside (Depart-ment of the Environment, 1990). These conflicts are complex. They change over time, and they often arise from forces and trends originating far away from the locality in question. Whatever the outcome of these conflicts, it is usually the people who live in the rural areas who have the least amount of say and influence over what happens.

Problems affecting rural people

The above issues are ones which are either distinctly rural, or they have a special impact on rural areas. Added to these must be a longer list of issues affecting groups and individuals within commu-nities, which will also be familiar in non-rural environments. The following are some of the main examples:

(i) *Poverty and deprivation.* Peter Townsend's study of poverty in the United Kingdom found that, 'The proportion in poverty or on its margins was as high or nearly as high in rural as in different groups of urban areas, despite the higher proportion of the rich in such areas' (Townsend, 1979, p. 563). A subsequent study by Brian McLaughlin and his team (1985), which was sponsored by the Department of the Environment, found quite a pervasive level of poverty in rural England; between 25 and 30 per cent of residents in five contrasting English rural areas were found to be at or below the then Supplementary Benefit level. We suspect that poverty elsewhere in the rural UK is at least as marked as in England, and significantly more so in parts of Northern Ireland. Furthermore, all the evidence points to a slight worsening of the position of the least well-off in the UK since the 1970s.

Poverty is not just a problem in itself: it is often associated with a number of other factors of disadvantage, such as poor housing, poor health, lower levels of educational achievement and powerlessness.

(ii) *Unemployment and under-employment.* The UK's significant internal variations in unemployment are regional rather than urban or rural. Unemployment is at a high level (over 15 per cent) in many rural parts of the UK distant from southern England, and particularly severe in the remoter parts of Northern Ireland. Underemployment and seasonal unemployment are also rife in agricultural and tourist areas where people 'make do' with part-time jobs and casual labour due to the unavailability of permanent full-time work.

(iii) *Housing.* The nature of the housing problem varies across the UK. In the more accessible rural areas, closer to the towns and cities, it is a problem of availability, brought about by wealthier incomers outbidding poorer locals on the open housing market. For those people in rural areas on low incomes, the housing situation has reached crisis point. At the same time, despite enormous advances in public-sector-led housing improvements throughout the UK, there remains a considerable stock of sub-standard housing (particularly privately rented and owner-occupied housing) in many remoter areas. Housing-availability is also a problem in those remoter areas which are popular with tourists and retired people.

(iv) *Health and disability.* It is a fallacy to believe that an attractive rural environment, in contrast to a decaying inner-city area, must foster good health. The incidence of mental, physical and sensory disabilities are comparable in rural and urban areas alike, and some areas experience particularly high levels of infant mortality, industry-related diseases etc. Especially further north in the UK, the harder climate, coupled with 'fuel poverty' and poorly insulated housing, creates an environment conducive to poor health and (for elderly people) hypothermia.

(v) *Social disadvantage.* From the late 1970s a debate has developed about the nature, extent and causes of disadvantage among people in rural areas. 'Rural deprivation' has become a widely used, but very confusing, rallying-point to justify a variety of different, and often opposing, objectives. These have run from arguments about the size of the government subsidy for rural local authorities, to questions about the distribution of power among classes and communities within rural areas (McLaughlin, 1987).

We cannot do full justice to the literature here, but we would draw attention to a book by Lowe *et al.* (1986) which provides an overview and analysis of the topic. They argue that deprivation and welfare can be seen and approached from quite different ideological standpoints, depending on one's view of society (consensus or conflict), on the basis of problems (residual, institutional or structural) and hence one's politics. This range of perspectives gives rise to differing prescriptions focusing, for example, on helping the market to deliver the goods, or on intervening to protect the rights of minority groups, or on the state control of production and welfare. These, in turn, condition the different objectives of community development: it is not only *what* is done, but also *why* and *how* it is done.

Rural policy and development

Alongside the growth of concern for rural problems there have been two further related areas of interest. One of these has been the development of a specifically rural perspective to a wide range of existing policies, occupations and interventions: for example, land-use planning, youth work, the church's ministry. The motives behind this are varied. In some cases, it is a genuine wish to build up a range of knowledge, skills and techniques which are appropriate to the rural context; in other cases, as Brian McLaughlin (1987) has observed, it has been the exploitation of the 'rural bandwagon' by rural local authorities to secure more central government subsidy, not to improve services but to hold the local taxes at a low level.

The way in which the churches, notably the Church of England, have sought to engage with rural issues is particularly interesting. The two consultations carried out in the Diocese of Hereford in 1976 and 1986 are impressive examples of the Church seeking to engage with rural problems (Lewis and Talbot-Ponsonby, 1987), and Russell (1986) provides a useful overview of the parish perspective. Given this sort of evidence, it would not be accurate to suggest that the decision to set up the Archbishops' Commission on Rural Areas was simply following in the wake of the hard-hitting report on urban deprivation, *Faith in the City*, produced by the Archbishop's Commission on Urban Priority Areas (1985). On the contrary, there has been a growing awareness among church leaders of the particular problems facing rural areas. The Commission's report, *Faith in the Countryside* (1990) must be read in that context.

The second area of growth has been an interest in the concept of rural development: or, rather, the concepts, as there is a diversity of interpretations. Rural development can mean a set of policies or the practices of certain types of agency or certain defined outcomes or certain types of process. Within the UK there is no consistent understanding of rural development and, even within the realm of central government agencies, there are enormous contrasts between different regions in the extent to which these various agencies are pursuing 'rural development'. For example, of the four 'countries' of the UK, only England has a long-established government agency specialising in rural development for all of its rural areas (the Rural Development Commission), while the coverage is only partial in Scotland (Highlands and Islands Enterprise) and Wales (Development Board for Rural Wales), and a state-sponsored agency has only begun to take shape in Northern Ireland in the 1990s. It is also interesting to observe that most UK government-sponsored rural development has taken the form of providing physical infrastructure (factories, roads, hotels, etc.) more than investing directly in the people themselves.

Community work must take a strong interest in rural development for several reasons:

—— While community development focuses upon localities and small groups of people, the changes which affect local people must be seen and tackled in a wider context which not only brings community groups into relationships with outside agencies, but also uses local action to confront the structural aspects of society.

—— Community development is not a panacea to the needs of rural society and rural areas, and so community work needs to operate alongside, and relate to, a variety of other interventions: agricultural support, land-use planning, social work, adult education, enterprise training.

—— There is a lot of rural development policy and practice which excludes local people from its formulation and implementation, and which can actually reinforce or perpetuate inequalities and other problems in rural areas; community development can provide a balance to the imposition of solutions by outside agencies.

—— Community work can help local people to take control of the concept and practice of rural development, defining it on their own terms.

In the introduction to their book on rural development, Henry Buller and Sue Wright (eds, 1990) identify the following key features of development:

(1) It is a *process*... which must be accumulative and must bring not just an improvement in physical and social conditions but also durable gains in people's abilities to control and sustain the conditions.

(2) It is about *betterment* and not just any change. Common threads would include: improvement in people's well-being; gains in people's access to the means to sustain the improvement; and improvements in self-determination.

(3) It must be *targetted on groups or classes of people*. This requires the correct identification of the target group. It may need to transform an incoherent category of people into an organised group. It must recognise that conflict will happen, as one group gains resources or power at the expense of another group, and that improvements for one group might involve a hindrance (or complete blocking) of improvements for others. It is also possible that the target group will change or even break up as new and possibly wider alliances or relationships develop.

(4) It is *personally and ideologically value-laden*, which means that opinions will differ about what constitutes development, and what is a desirable end-state.

This formulation is helpful because it gives a means of evaluating the wide range of policies and initiatives (many of them with a pronounced land-use or economic focus) in terms of their contribution to rural development. It also shows the central contribution which community development should be making, by placing a proper emphasis upon people, processes, and the distribution of resources and power.

David Thomas has shown how community work contributes to wider development through two linked processes:

—— The development of communal coherence, which involves developing relationships and networks (within communities, and with agencies and networks), attitudes (what people know and feel about each other), and people's roles: '...to help people know and interact with each other in a variety of roles at the point of residence', which is the community

—— Enhancing 'people's sense of political and welfare responsibility, through which they take a more active and responsible part in political processes and in processes of social provision and control' (Thomas, 1983, p. 98)

We believe that these concepts help to fill a gap in the rural development system in the UK which in the past, with some exceptions, has had a very ambivalent view of the role which people and communities should play in the process. Rural development is an arid and ineffective exercise if it is preoccupied with physical infrastructural provision, investment in narrow economic sectors and the imposition of policies by central and local government agencies. This preoccupation is at best incomplete but, worse still, it runs the risk of further disadvantaging the people and localities which should be the prime beneficiaries.

It is because of these risks that community development agencies and individual workers have fought shy of becoming too involved in essentially top-down and repressive forms of rural development (Ann Meadows, 1985). To be effective, 'community involvement' must not be some peripheral process, serving to legitimise a predetermined programme or to add a little icing to the cake. Rural development must have at its core the active development of people and communities for them to take on the role of planners, decision-makers and key actors and, ultimately, to be the prime beneficiaries. Rural development should not only be about creating jobs, saving schools, building houses, delivering neighbourly care or improving the environment; it should also be concerned about promoting and sustaining an active and responsible citizenship, encouraging people to lead fulfilling lives, ensuring people acquire greater power and self-determination (especially among those who are most disadvantaged) and generally securing a more just and fair society.

Rural community work has a key contribution to make by drawing together the functional notions of better and more jobs, services and resources, with the developmental notions of participation, mutual support, equality and responsibility. The focus for this action is the neighbourhood or community, the local social system where people live, work and play out their daily lives. And, as Ann Meadows (personal communication, 1985) has made clear, 'the community' for the community worker means something more than simply the place where people live, or a source of untapped voluntary labour: it is the entity on which to focus attention, resources and concern. Development of the community as a coherent (though not necessarily homogeneous or consensual) unit therefore becomes an important and worthwhile goal in its own right.

2

Communities and People in Rural Areas

Community work is concerned with helping people to work together in their community, to grow in confidence and competence, in order to tackle their priorities and needs. This requires the community worker to understand both what is meant by 'community' and the nature of the specific community with which he or she is engaging.

Sociologists and other social scientists have used 'community' as a concept and object of study in order to shed light on the nature of social relationships both within this defined unit, and also more widely in society. In contrast, policy-makers have often used 'community' in an imprecise or flexible way, sometimes to imply a small locality, or to reflect a less formal and less institutional setting, or as a 'warmer' way of referring to the general public.

However, the community is something more than a collection of individual people and households in a locality. It is a 'local social system', linking individuals together to varying degrees in a complexity of relationships and roles. The individuals have a personal responsibility for their own actions and attitudes but it is important in a community that they also have a collective, corporate responsibility for ensuring that appropriate relationships exist, and that there is justice, fairness, and peace (ACORA, 1990, p. 22).

Community workers should be committed to the idea of community for two very practical reasons:

---- Communities, and groups within them, are executive agencies in their own right: they can and should plan and take action to meet the needs and priorities which they themselves

17

identify. They are not merely the passive recipients of services and resources dispensed from outside.

—— Communities are the social units which the worker seeks to develop in terms of such qualities as people's awareness and responsiveness to issues, their sense of confidence and effectiveness, their ability to empower and redistribute resources towards disadvantaged people, and their ability to foster mutual aid and interdependence.

In this chapter, our aim is to give a flavour of what people may find in rural communities, and to look at some of the different perspectives. Effective community work requires the bringing-together of first-hand experience and observation with material derived from theory and research. The knowledge and understanding which comes from face-to-face contact with the community, is complemented and built upon by what we can understand and perceive more generally about communities. The added insight which theory and research can give is especially important for many rural community workers who, due to large geographical areas and quantities of villages with which to work, cannot always devote the time to become sufficiently immersed in, and knowledgeable about, each of the communities with which they are working.

There are striking contrasts between different rural parts of the country. The commuter village of 5000 people, twenty miles from London, where there is an almost urban level of shops and other services, is manifestly different from the agricultural village in Northern Ireland of 200 people, remote from Belfast and Derry, with a shop and a pub and looking little different from the way it did fifty years ago. Similarly, the ex-industrial villages of North-East England and South Wales with their high unemployment and their decaying environment, stand in contrast to the 'chocolate-box' conservation area villages of the Lake District or Dorset, where the only sign of problems appears to be the odd piece of litter dropped by a passing tourist, or an occasional untidy front garden.

Yet, superficial observations are deceptive. Our casual observations will have overlooked the hidden 25 per cent of households in the otherwise affluent commuter village who are living in poverty and are forced by economic reality and social stigma to lead a lonely, home-centred existence, away from the village squash and aerobics clubs, the daily coffee mornings, the dinner parties and Women's Institute. The Fermanagh village, in many ways a last bastion of traditional rural life, hides the deep-rooted and lasting rural and economic effects brought about by 'the troubles' in Northern Ireland since the early 1970s: Protestants not co-operating with their Catholic neighbours, and a prevailing government policy which tends to stifle local initiative for fear of fomenting unrest. The old folks in the Durham mining village, who will not leave their homes at night-time – not because of the cold climate but because of their fear of crime, against themselves or their property, and who now feel like aliens in a community which once they understood and felt part of – are not so very different from their counterparts in the Dorset village.

The point is that, when we talk about rural communities, we are referring to complex and changing social systems. There *are* differences throughout the United Kingdom, but there are also very marked differences between communities nearby and also between people *within* each community. The complexity of all this means that almost every generalisation is open to challenge, but at the same time we can find areas of similarity in otherwise apparently contrasting situations.

Every rural community is unique, and community workers must be sensitive to its individuality, but there are general lessons which workers should take account of, and use to inform the way in which they carry out their work.

Rural communities

However dispassionate we attempt to be in viewing a community as an object and instigator of development, there is no doubt that community, especially when prefixed by 'rural', is a powerful and emotive concept. To some people it conjures up visions of care and social harmony, to others it is a means of social control and perpetuation of patterns of inequality.

The idea of community includes notions of reciprocal human relationships, voluntary effort, interest in local affairs, neighbourliness: above all, the village is seen as a place where everybody knows and cares for each other. This 'rural romanticism' is often placed in contrast to life in towns and cities, where the feeling of community is said to be low or non-existent.

However, sociologists and others have been at pains to point out the shortcomings of this simplistic view. Writers such as Newby (1980), Abrams (1980) and Williams (1973) have illustrated the poverty, stifling relationships and disruption which nineteenth-century industrialisation brought to the village and, even in the 1950s, Smith and Bate (1953) emphasised the enormous variations in neighbourliness and feelings of community between different villages. Pahl (1966) has argued that community feelings are more related to people's social class and the stage in their life-cycle, than to whether they live in a rural or urban setting.

If we continue to use the word 'community' to describe the sum-total of people and relationships in modern-day villages in the UK, we must be aware that we are not necessarily using it in a traditional sense, nor indeed that we are talking about the same thing throughout the UK. Based largely upon lowland England, Anthony Russell has written:

> The contemporary village can be seen as a social entity comprised of a series of identifiable, and increasingly separate, interest groups. In short, the modern village is a community of communities comprised of groups of people who have different understandings about the nature of the village and the future of the countryside. Village life today is the product of the interaction between these groups, with their different understandings of the nature and function of the modern village. (Russell, 1986)

On the whole, we agree with this concept of groups-within-communities, even though it is doubtful how far one can push the idea of uniformity/communality within the groups, and the idea that all residents can in some way be slotted into a group. We also need to bear in mind that 'rural community' does not necessarily mean 'village', in the sense of a nucleated cluster of dwellings. Particularly in Scotland and Ireland, but also in parts of England and Wales, villages are less common, and scatterings of individual dwellings over considerable areas of 10 square miles or more are common. This has implications both for the operation of the 'community' and, in turn, for the community worker's practice.

We need to avoid the trap of understanding community only in spatial terms. This is a theme emphasised by several authors of rural community studies, who opt for a theory of social networks (Stacey, 1969). One effect of the increase in the number of incomers has been to raise the importance of networks both *within* particular localities and *across* geographical communities. The experience of the diocese of Hereford, which undertook a consultation on rural matters, undoubtedly reflects a widespread phenomenon:

It seems that there is a growing significance in these 'network' communities. People who are linked by a common interest, meet and spend time together, sometimes travelling considerable distances to do so. (Lewis and Talbot-Ponsonby, 1987)

This theme is also reflected in *Faith in the Countryside*:

a community is one whose people draw together to express their relatedness by focusing on things they have in common. Traditionally, this used to be centred around the land, and around farming as an activity, a work pattern and a way of life. Yet any group which shares concerns, norms, patterns of mutual support, is a community. So it is possible to build communities which look very different from those of the past and yet which give people space to grow and be enriched. (ACORA, 1990, p. 23)

Many rural communities have changed out of all recognition from what they were, and the people within them, whether locals or newcomers, may also be different. But this does not undermine the need to make efforts to develop the community into something worthwhile, to be concerned with 'those principles so crucial for communal life – justice, corporate responsibility, protection of the disadvantaged' based upon neighbourliness, love, compassion and mutual care (ACORA, 1990, pp. 23–4).

People in rural communities

With the spread of influences such as television and mass education, and with improved mobility and accessibility, it is sometimes argued that, beyond the obvious geographical factor of location, there is no longer any such thing as a rural culture or way of life. Rural communities are felt to be a cross-section of national society who just happen to live in villages and hamlets. Traditional rural society may still exist at the geographical margins, but the people and networks in most villages are not so very different from their counterparts in towns.

To an extent, we agree. In most rural areas, one is likely to find a mixture of people: different social classes; markedly different levels of wealth; different backgrounds, values and aspirations; different levels of education; different ages; different religions and other beliefs; different group affiliations; different levels of needs and ability. However, we believe that it is still possible to identify distinctive local cultures and personal characteristics which are rural in character. These characteristics are less discernible in the accessible rural areas around most cities than further afield, but they are still there. Therefore, the generalisations which follow about people's identification with, and participation in, rural community life are a product of two main factors: a traditional, rural set of characteristics and tendencies; and a general, nationwide set of characteristics and tendencies. The extent to which they interact, and what comes out as a result, will vary from community to community.

Cultural characteristics

(i) *Conservatism.* Many community workers who have experience of urban communities are quick to identify the low expectations, slow adjustment to change, and the limited experience of collective action in rural communities.

The hesitancy of rural communities in actively addressing problems associated with change is explained by complex historical and social forces. Newby has explored extensively the deference of nineteenth-century farmworkers to landowners; it was at the heart of the social order and its influence on rural society remains to this day: 'The landowner has long relied on a traditional sense of deference in rural society and has conferred a sense of identity and place in return' (Newby, 1977).

When we talk about tradition and stability of rural communities we are using shorthand to refer to a powerful social system shaped over centuries. It is this which accounts for the importance of traditional social networks.

It begins also to explain the hold of Conservative Party political philosophy in the shires of England. The affluent middle-class incomers have reduced the power of the established landowning, business and farming interests, but often they share the same priorities. The position of the poor and powerless has not changed.

Absorbing the extent of conservative attitudes in rural Britain is essential for community workers. This is a central theme developed by Graham Benfield in his analysis of nine projects in rural England: 'The established leadership, even when it acquiesced in the intervention of the worker, had little time, interest or motivation in becoming involved in new initiatives beyond an extension of its existing roles' (Benfield, 1990).

Resistance or reluctance to change permeates many facets of rural life, including local government and attitudes towards voluntary organisations. The hold of conservatism is illustrated in the analysis by Williams (1984) of local government response to the six rural development research projects (1977–9) set up to seek 'low cost solutions in areas not currently statutorily provided':

> There was considerable opposition from the Association of District Councils, and the Association of County Councils to the concept of community development, both arguing that such appointments might stir up unrealistic demands for services that could not be met.

Even where local authorities employ community workers, such as the Scottish Regional Councils, there remains a mistrust of processes which raise people's aspirations above local, low-cost initiatives.

For those community workers who would normally wish to adopt a radical stance, the ability to work creatively within the dominant conservatism of shire counties presents a major challenge. This becomes most evident when a campaigning organisation which is not middle-class-dominated emerges. We need to know and influence the strategies and tactics used by such organisations, if they are to be effective in what are essentially conservative rural communities. At the same time it is crucial for community workers to find ways of achieving results by operating within the consensus framework of those communities.

(ii) *Self-sufficiency and self-help.* There are many instances across the UK of villagers maintaining halls and community centres through voluntary effort. Although these buildings have sometimes received some central or local government funding, there are frequent examples of a small hall or centre which literally had been built by local people. A determination to have a communal facility has overridden obstacles and disappointments placed in their way, and they have done everything themselves. Alongside this form of primary self-help goes a capacity to raise funds. The extent and ingenuity of this can be forbidding when the small size of population is considered. Events are held on a regular basis, and often form an important part of a community's social activities.

The tradition of self-help among people in rural communities is undoubtedly strong. It relates in part to the sense of neglect by public authorities that more remote communities have experienced, the feeling that very little will happen unless you do it yourselves. In some areas it can be crucial to a community's survival: people need each other at different times of the year, lending tools or equipment for example, or providing the necessary labour force to get a job done. Here, self-help amounts to much more than a collective wish to improve social, recreational facilities. In some instances people will band together because they are offended by what they see as attempts by outsiders to write-off their community; the revival of Allenheads, a Pennine village of 165 people in Northumberland, has been attributed to this feeling of pride and determination (see Lumb, 1990). Or self-help can help to counter a feeling of fatalism within some rural communities, a sense that they are in the grip of profound forces which they cannot control – a theme explored by Brody (1973) in his analysis of the connections between family farms, local communities and decline in the west of Ireland.

An equally powerful aspect of the self-help tradition is its overlay with social relationships and leadership in villages. Many schemes and organisations which depend on a small number of people for their existence provide a focal point for further social interaction. Given that, in most rural communities, the small population size means that only a limited number of groups and organisations can be established, the tendency will be for existing leaders and 'gatekeepers' to play a dominant role. The relative lack of alternative groups means that if people are not part of one of the few groups which do exist, whether through choice or exclusion, they will probably not be part of the community, and will therefore be very isolated. Thus it is misleading to imagine that self-help opens up opportunities for pluralism and participation in rural communities. Quite the reverse: in the majority of cases the self-help tradition will reinforce the existing social system.

(iii) *Minorities, attitudes and power.* One product of the conservatism and self-help ethos of rural society which we have outlined above is the role of groups or, more precisely, of different categories of people within rural communities. For some, rural life presents the best of all worlds: clean air, space, a comfortable home, an attractive environment, a haven from the fast pace of life in the city, and a reasonably friendly community. This is particularly the case for those who are comfortable, wealthy, mobile, able-bodied, articulate, well educated, white and male.

For others, the tightness of rural society, combined with its relative lack of local opportunities and its remoteness from the towns and cities, can be a stifling and repressive environment. Personal circumstances and prevailing attitudes often interplay to produce a subtle but complex pattern of relative disadvantage, powerlessness and opportunity denied.

Readers wishing to learn more about this should refer to some of the many writings, mainly by rural sociologists: Newby (1977), Russell (1986), McLaughlin (1986), Little (1987). *Faith in the Countryside* has identified those particularly important elements which determine or differentiate qualities of life for people in rural areas: age, gender and wealth (ACORA, 1990).

For teenagers, the lack of easy access to facilities and resources for work and leisure produce their own hardships, but these can be made worse in those rural cultures which fail or refuse to recognise young people's aspirations and their need to develop a wider experience of life. Here, older and more powerful members of the community – parents, the parish council, the church elders, etc. – are unsympathetic to the needs of young people, and try to suppress their desire for material opportunities and the means of self-expression which depart from the norm.

At the other end of the scale, some elderly people are in a very comfortable position, with a secure and ample pension, low financial overheads, a car, and the wherewithal to take an active part in local village life. For others, who may be subsisting on a minimal pension, becoming frailer in health, and totally dependent on a declining range of services and public transport, life in the rural community can be an isolating and increasingly worrying experience.

For a woman, life in the countryside can be more fulfilling and sociable than living on a suburban estate or in an inner-city tower block. However, it can also be a limiting experience: lonely, remote from facilities or from jobs which can give self-respect as well as some economic independence, boring and oppressive. The material difficulties of rural life for women can be further exacerbated by prevailing attitudes in the rural culture. While some rural societies are matriarchal, and place the older family woman in a position of respect, power and influence, a more common situation is of women being placed in a subordinate position to men, with little room given for self-expression, exercise of power or even equality of decision-making within the household.

Wealth and disposable income may or may not earn respect in the rural community, but it is a strong determinant of power and of the ability to lead the fulfilling life of one's choice.

Community identity

Community-based action is more likely where there is a strong sense of community identity and/or well-developed social linkages within a locality. Documented evidence on this theme is not easy to find, but in the late 1960s research done in England for the Redcliffe-Maud Commission showed that most rural residents *could* identify a 'home area', that 85 per cent of them saw their home areas as being no larger than a parish or ward, and that 76 per cent felt that they *belonged* to that home area.

It has been observed that the feeling of community identity is greater in villages which are nucleated rather than dispersed, and in villages which have a primary school (Connor, 1977). Other focal points which community workers have found to be important include: the pub, shop, church/chapel, and village hall/community centre.

People's personal circumstances are also known to condition their attachment to their home area: in particular, attachment increases with one's length of residence in the area, and among those of lower socio-economic status (Redcliffe-Maud, 1969). Newby's (1977) research with farm workers in Suffolk found that those workers who felt least attached to a community lived in isolation outside villages, on farms, or lived in what amounted to social ghettoes within villages, as an 'encapsulated community'.

In those communities where a sense of common identity is not apparent, it may be necessary for a community worker to help develop it. Clearly, that will not happen overnight. It is more a question of giving recognition to the issue and of building on what is there.

Involvement in community activities

Despite popular images of the rural village as a place where everybody is active in helping everybody else, the evidence suggests that the rural picture is not so very different from other environments. Research undertaken in the 1970s (BBC, 1978) showed that leisure patterns and church attendance in rural areas were almost identical to town and city situations.

More recently, the periodic General Household Survey reveals that leisure time is increasingly non-communal (especially watching TV at home, or reading), and overall levels of caring for the community and for individuals continue to decline. Surprisingly, the 1981 survey found that:

> groups which might be expected to have more time available, such as people without children, the unemployed, and perhaps the recently retired show lower than average participation rates in voluntary work.

Nevertheless, the middle aged and middle class do figure pro-minently among volunteers. Women are slightly more likely than men to do voluntary work at least once a week. The survey showed that 27 per cent of people doing voluntary work in Great Britain do it 'informally', i.e. not carried out through any sort of voluntary or statutory organisation.

Being aware of these and other sources of data, and being able to access them, is important in community work. It helps to build expertise and confidence, and it equips staff to speak with authority on a general matter about which most people have opinions.

Political action

Community-based action, especially where it extends beyond voluntary self-help activities within the neighbourhood, is 'political', although many rural people would not actually view it that way. Campaigns to fight against the closure of the village primary school, or against the introduction of open-cast mining on one's doorstep, or to push for the building of a by-pass road, are all political, whether or not they engage in party politics. In order to take political action, people need not only to be aware of the issue or need. They must know and understand 'the system', they must be sufficiently motivated to take action, they must have some skill to put their ideas into practice. Lastly, they need to manage the actions: e.g. bringing together people and resources, changing tactics in the light of changing circumstances, knowing when to step up or relax the pressure.

Surveys (e.g. Redcliffe-Maud, 1969) have shown that rural people generally have a higher level of complacency for their circumstances, they have less awareness about the system (i.e. who does what and how decisions are taken) and less confidence in their abilities to get things changed. Those who are 'in the know' are in a considerably better position to work the system not only to their own advantage, but also at times intentionally to the detriment of others. The likelihood that rural people will organise themselves collectively to take action is therefore generally less than in urban areas. However, this is not universally true. The possibility of collective political action increases with people's socio-economic status and with levels of education, and is greater among men than women, i.e. it varies according to the mixture of individuals within the community, and not just the nature of the community itself.

People's background, culture and values are also extremely relevant. The implication of Howard Newby's work on the deferential culture of the rural working class in East Anglia (Newby, 1977) is that people are prepared to tolerate quite exceptionally poor living conditions rather than challenge the authority and policies of leadership both locally and at local government level. Anthony Russell (1986) follows a similar theme. He distinguishes between the rural locals, who belong to and identify with the community but feel no strong need to get involved actively in community affairs, and the incomers who seek acceptance by the community through active participation and getting things done. Lest this view is assumed to be a lowland English view, we found similar traits in Wales, Scotland and (to a lesser extent) Northern Ireland.

However, culture is not just a matter of the physical environment in which people grow up. Thirty years ago Almond and Verba (1963) found from a large survey of the United Kingdom that people's ability and likelihood of participating in political action was closely related to the participatory nature of their family upbringing, their school life and their work life, and their experience in voluntary organisations was particularly crucial. Therefore, in rural deferential cultures, where there is little participation in decision-making at home, at school or at work, and few voluntary organisations, the community worker is less likely to find the community able and willing to get organised to address even those issues which they know to be important.

Religion, too, can be an important aspect of this culture. For example, rural community workers in Northern Ireland have pointed to the stronger tradition of collective community action among Catholics than among Protestants, with the implication that Protestants need to 'get their community act together' more effectively if they are not to lose out on the resources on offer (for a discussion of this question, see M. Fitzduff, 1990). In rural Wales, community workers have pointed to the paradox of the non-conformist ('chapel') culture which did so much to promote social improvement and equality in the past, but whose egalitarian ethic now is impeding progress in villages by deterring the emergence of individual leaders and innovators from the rural community. It is being left to incomers to take the lead, which itself is not always welcomed.

The history of the community is also crucial. Community workers operating in areas which in the past have been dominated by a single paternalistic employer have noted that local residents are often not easily disposed to taking collective action to meet their needs, because they have been largely dependent on an all-providing benevolent institution. Examples abound throughout the UK: the coal-mining areas of South Wales and northern England, the estate villages of England and Scotland, and the remote housing estates built by oil companies (see Justad, 1990) and Ministry of Defence, to name some of the most obvious ones. The crunch comes when change is foisted on to the community: a coal-mine closes, or the country estate is broken up and sold off in order to pay debts or death duties. The community are ill-prepared to accommodate the change, and it may be many years before they acquire even the basic levels of responsibility and self-reliance which are taken for granted in most rural areas.

Groups within rural communities

If we now look inside a rural community, what are we likely to find? What are the groups and institutions? Who is in them? How and why do they operate, and relate to each other? Who is not included, and what does this mean for the distribution of power and resources within communities?

Particularly in those rural communities based upon agriculture, social networks based upon farmers, or upon farm workers, have existed for many years. During the nineteenth century, particularly in the arable farming areas, where much hired labour was required, the rural community was largely a working-class community, with most of the farming employers living outside the village. The working class were linked in what Howard Newby has described as an 'occupational community':

It was sustained by the isolation of the rural village, by the strong kinship links between the village inhabitants and by the need for co-operation in times of family crises. Most importantly, it was forged out of the overlap between workplace and village, the fact that, as an occupational community, relationships established at work spilled over into leisure hours, while the accepted code of behaviour which was followed in the village also applied to the situation at work. (Newby, 1977)

In many parts of the UK there are still agricultural occupational communities today: less so now in the arable farming areas, but in livestock and upland farming areas. To some extent, it is a concept which also applies to other occupational communities in certain rural areas: fishermen, coal-miners, slate quarrymen. However, most of these are in a state of change, as employment levels in these industries have fallen, a trend which has been reflected in the dramatic fall in membership of the Agricultural and Allied Workers' Union and National Union of Mineworkers in recent years.

It is important for the community worker to understand the traditions of rural social groups if she or he is to work effectively and sensitively with them. For example, in the Scottish Highlands and Islands a community worker told us about the importance of understanding how local people in her area took decisions. It was based not on the formalities of a community meeting but on a slow process of mulling-over an idea, in turn, by senior members of the kinship networks. To try to force the pace with a proposal, or to try and get a binding decision through an alternative community structure, was likely to end in failure for the community worker.

It is possible to identify groups in a number of ways: for example, membership (or non-membership) of particular community organisations such as the church, women's institute, youth club, parish/ community council or playgroup, or by people's characteristics such as social class, occupation, religion, family ties, ethnic background, age or patterns of behaviour. These characteristics can have significance in tying people together into social groups and, as important, in differentiating them from other people in the same community. The distinction between locals and newcomers, which is a commonly held 'division' in many rural communities, should be treated with caution, because it has been used as a device to reduce working-class activism by focusing their attention on a perceived threat from 'outsiders', away from class conflicts *within* the indigenous rural social system.

As well as the existence of groups within communities, another important aspect is the relationship between them: whether they are mutually supportive or in conflict, whether their membership is exclusive, how they overlap, what roles people take in them.

In some parts of Britain there is a startling integration between many of the organisations in the sense that (a) they work closely together and (b) a large number of individuals are involved with more than one organisation. For example, when we visited the island of Skye, the voluntary organisations were busy organising the annual fund-raising fair; and volunteers and staff of the various agencies were all involved in supporting the event. In addition it became clear that a handful of the key individuals were active in several voluntary activities – the council of social service, the church and running the local WEA branch for example.

In other parts of the country there is evidence of severe disloca-tion between groups and organisations, and the professionals keep their distance – metaphorically – from voluntary activities. Further-more, there is a separation in participation: some people belong to one organisation, some to another, and there is little communica-tion between them. Examples of this picture can be found in commuter areas where the number of new incomers has been particularly high.

Implications for rural community work

Rural communities are as complex and as variable as the people in them, and nowadays, more than ever before, villages are inhabited by a mixture of indigenous people and newcomers, rich and poor, concerned and apathetic, confident and unsure, young and old, able-bodied and handicapped, involved and alienated, and a whole host of other contrasting characteristics.

Needs, and the disposition to do something about them, are not evenly distributed among all residents, any more than the distribu-tion of power and resources. The pressures of change, which for many rural communities have only become obvious in the second half of the twentieth century, do not bear evenly on the whole community. Any differences of view over priorities and policies, which stem from different cultural positions, are exacerbated and emphasised. The community worker is thus faced with a complexity of needs, relationships, contrasting abilities, attitudes and activities.

In urban areas, neighbourhoods may be *relatively* homogeneous in their composition, such that the community worker knows that by working in a particular locality s/he is working with disadvan-taged people. However, it is dangerous to make such assumptions in rural areas. A group which is active in the rural community, such as

a parish/community council or women's institute, may be a demo-
cratic and progressive agent of change, or a repressive and conservative defender of existing patterns of inequality. Professionals
with ascribed leadership roles, such as the clergyman or teacher,
may similarly be a concerned and active force in the community, or
a guardian of the status quo. It is a key challenge to the rural
community worker to identify and assess these structures and
individuals, and take account of them in a community work
strategy which is specific to a community at a point in time.

At the same time he or she can make use of a check list of key
political points in order to attempt to understand where power lies
in a community:

——   Who are the *leaders*? In which organisations are they active?
——   Who are the '*gatekeepers*', those who, for example, sanction
         entry of newcomers to particular groups?
——   Where are there social, economic or political *cliques*?
——   Which are the dominant *families*, historically and socially?

Looking for clues to these and other points should help community workers to understand groups and organisations. They can
assess their significance. Equally important, they can obtain a more
rounded picture of the established, formal organisations – such as
the women's institute – and the more fluid, informal groups – such
as the family networks, and the women who assemble at the school
gates to collect their children every afternoon – and the connections
(in terms of membership and leadership) between them.

We are not suggesting that community workers should deploy
social science tools for this kind of assessment. It is a 'lighter', more
impressionistic analysis we think is required. The same would be
true when cross-relating the membership and role of community
groups and voluntary organisations to the established political
institutions – the District Council and County Council. How well
community workers are able to understand complex and intricate
relationships will often be a major determinant of their capacity to
practise effectively. This is because, while they may want to
concentrate on working with the apparently weaker, less formal
groups – or with people who do not belong to any groups – they
may be obliged to keep the communication channels open with the
more established groups and political structures. We think that this
form of 'permission seeking' is a distinguishing feature of rural
community work.

The rural situation is significant. The degree of isolation creates its own problems for individuals, and also emphasises differences in people's ability to accommodate them: people's personal mobility (which may be connected to car ownership, wealth, or public transport availability) and personal confidence and competence are crucially important to their ability to overcome the problems of isolation and to participate in community life. However, this is more than a question of resources and personality: social accept-ability is a further consideration. For example, as the Norfolk REPLAN programme which attempted to bring educational op-portunities to unemployed adults has observed:

> Unemployed people in rural areas are isolated . . . They live in physically isolated communities and, being unemployed in them, you are even more isolated. There is little social acceptance of being unemployed, so it is difficult to meet people who admit to being unemployed. (REPLAN Review, March 1989)

Thus, those people in rural areas who are marginalised – the unemployed, poor, homeless, ethnic minorities, travellers – may be multiply disadvantaged in terms of involvement: they do not have the resources to attend meetings etc., they are not accepted by the majority population, and they may be ill-disposed to organise themselves collectively (see Scott *et al.*, 1991).

The rural situation is also significant in presenting dilemmas to the community worker. If we take the example of local rural culture, we believe that it is a feature of the community which should be cherished. By helping local people to investigate it and learn about it, they will appreciate more vividly their roots and pride of place, they may see more clearly where they want to go and they will have a valued tradition which they can demonstrate – and even 'sell' – to outsiders. However, this same culture may have stifled social and sexual equality, and even accentuated conflict with different cultures in the same locality. The challenge to the community worker then is to help groups within communities to value the past, but to use it wisely and selectively as a key to the future.

Every group and gatekeeper/leader may be an asset or a con-straint. A community with no apparent groups or leaders may present an impossibly blank wall for the community worker looking for a point of entry: someone to talk to and through whom to facilitate action. However, it may not be much help in an apparently 'active' community with a parish council, women's institute, church, chapel, school, pub, shop, youth club, playgroup, etc. if all of these institutions are dominated by powerful and repressive elites; even more so, when there is considerable overlap of membership between these institutions.

Herein lies a further dilemma. The bread-and-butter basis of community work lies in working with groups, whether they are already in existence or specially formed in order to further some community development objectives. However, as we have observed earlier, collective community activity is not commonplace among rural people – as a result of a sense of shyness and a long tradition of individualism. The community worker needs to face up to working with this cultural reality. Even where groups exist, the importance of working with individuals has a pragmatic signif- icance, as Jackie Denman described in Herefordshire:

> It was important to establish long-term relationships with indi- viduals and to build up their trust... It seemed clear to me from an early stage that there was not going to be much progress from working with organised groups 'in session'. Somehow there is much more resistance to outside influence and to change in general from a group, and they are slow to change collectively. I found a much more effective way of working to be to concentrate on individuals who in turn could exercise a long- term influence over organisations. (Hereford and Worcester RCC, 1981)

The importance of working 'with the grain' of rural society has been stressed by Clem McCartney (1990). He points to the 'traditional modes of discourse' by which the old rural communi- ties discussed matters and reached conclusions:

> Issues are tackled obliquely by informal groups in the home, the pub or at the market, through apparently desultory talk which seems very repetitive and inconsequential. But this is a process of considering and becoming familiar with the dimensions of an issue until a sense of the right response becomes clear.

Community workers must recognise this as a starting point, but then challenge those involved to develop it into new 'flexible modes of discourse' more appropriate to the pressure and pace of change which now impact upon rural communities. This, he suggests, requires sensitivity to the subtleties of the community, an appro- priately long period of time for the development process and a preparedness to work through and evolve informal networks and groups which fit in with the culture of the community.

The rural community worker, while promoting and working towards communal and participatory ideals, will find her/himself needing to work with and through a variety of individuals:

—— gatekeepers who can facilitate the worker's entry into particular networks in the community

—— people in authority who have access to key resources – human, material and financial

—— people in greater need, who may or may not be part of an established group

—— people on the margins who may not otherwise benefit or be contacted by less direct approaches through the community at large

It is essential for the community worker and his/her agency to take seriously the position of the individual in rural communities. We shall argue that the theme of working through individuals has major implications for the community worker's strategy because of observations such as that made by a Northern Ireland community worker:

> Country people seem to be less inclined towards organised group activity; their way of life seems to encourage individualism plus a shyness about belonging to or speaking in a group. (Conlon, 1977)

This chapter has served to alert the community worker to some more general aspects of people in communities in the United Kingdom, in which the boundaries and distinctions between urban and rural society are rapidly eroding. The purpose of doing this is to prepare the worker for what s/he may – or may not – observe at first hand when working in and with a rural community. The range of interpretations may be daunting, but we believe it is better for the worker to be conscious of them in advance, than to fall into a delicate community situation unprepared. Rural communities have a reputation for allowing freedom and individuality, but they also have long memories. It may take years or generations to heal rifts caused by apparently naive or innocent transgressions, and community workers do not have the time or resilience to live with this. This is why 'understanding the community' is a key skill and area of knowledge in rural community work.

3

Developing a Strategy

Increasingly, funders and managers are calling for a greater application of strategic principles to rural community work. This demand is accepted by many practitioners, who see it as an aid to their own thinking and self-management, and as a way of helping the communities themselves to understand and influence the process. However, others are suspicious of something which they fear will distract from the spontaneity and freshness of 'intuitive' practice. To an extent, we sympathise, but a strategy need not be complex, sophisticated or inflexible. It is simply a process of making sense of a situation, and mobilising effort and resources in ways which are appropriate.

Principles

(i) *Aims/purpose*. What are we really trying to achieve through our strategy? In Chapter 1 we saw that rural community work tends to have two sets of purposes, labelled as functional and developmental. These two main purposes are not necessarily incompatible. They do, however, demand that choices are made in a community work strategy, especially in the disposition of resources, the nature of help on offer, whom to work with and the balance between working directly with communities or working for them at a distance.

For example, if priority is to be given to a functional aim such as maximising the number of good-quality village halls, then the community work strategy may need to emphasise the provision of specialist technical advice on buildings, design, fund-raising, cash-flow management, charity law etc., and negotiating with and influencing grant aid providers. If, however, priority is to be given to a developmental aim such as the empowerment of young isolated women in rural areas, then the community work strategy may need to focus on one or a limited number of communities at any one time, and work at a more psychological and painstaking level to identify, encourage, cultivate and support a number of individuals, with no other predetermined agenda.

Making this choice of aims or purpose, and the balance between them, fundamentally influences subsequent detailed decisions in the strategy, and so must be confronted at an early stage. We make no judgement here of their relative value, other than to say that they are both important in rural community work.

(ii) *Ownership of the strategy.* Community work is concerned with local responsibility, communities taking control of their problems and solutions, and with local–central balances of power. It is therefore paradoxical if a community work strategy is evolved and managed externally to, and independently of, a community work constituency. It raises questions about the legitimacy of that strategy, and about the power which the strategy may exert over a constituency. In an ideal world, communities should own and control the community work strategy, and not just retain the right to accept or reject what is offered to them. While we defend this as a guiding principle, we accept the difficulties of securing this, especially in rural areas where:

—— a constituency is often enormous, such that effective involvement in the development of a community work strategy is impracticable

—— people are unfamiliar with the concept of community work, and cannot readily articulate their needs in this respect

—— people are unaccustomed to strategic planning, and so may not know how to make a useful input to the process

In practice, therefore, community involvement in the strategy may have to be achieved through such mechanisms as holding consultations with representatives of networks of community groups (e.g. associations of parish councils, youth councils or federations of Women's Institutes). More importantly, involvement can be achieved by actively encouraging a constituency to make demands on the worker and agency, to influence both the delivery of the strategy and the process of continuous adjustment and refinement which is important to strategic planning.

This issue of ownership and influence is not only significant in the strategies of agencies, it also applies to individual workers, especially voluntary activists who are operating within a single community and who often often have no clear contract or defined role within the community.

To develop a strategy, account should be taken of factors in three main spheres:

—— our own situation (whether 'we' are an individual worker or agency)
—— our constituency (by which we mean a particular target group, the community or range of communities)
—— other relevant actors/agencies

For each of these spheres, there is a diversity of factors such as needs, resources, abilities, values and expectations which we need to address. There are also some guiding principles which need to be clarified from the start, because they will significantly influence later strategic choices.

The situation of the agency

Several factors are relevant in this context: the permanence of the agency, its wider image and role, its geographical scale of operation, the time available – in addition to its culture, traditions and resources.

Permanence

A survey of community workers at the beginning of the 1980s (Francis *et al.*, 1984) showed that in rural areas just about every community work agency was permanent, i.e. not a short-term project. This reflected the relatively long-term and low-level nature of rural community work practice being carried out through rural community councils, councils of social/voluntary service, Scottish community education departments and Northern Ireland district councils. Since that survey, there has been a mushrooming of short-term (2–3 year) community work posts, and to a lesser extent the emergence of short-life agencies.

A considerable constituency, a track record, and an array of commitments and expectations are built up by an agency such as a long-established rural community council. This brings both assets and constraints from a strategic viewpoint. On the one hand, longevity brings a certain reliability, a legitimacy born from long experience, a place in the pecking-order of local agencies and authorities, and a diversity of contacts and relationships. On the other hand, this same longevity often brings a conservatism, difficulty in addressing new issues and new constituencies in new ways, and a reluctance to take hard decisions about priorities.

In contrast, a short-life agency or project may bring freshness and innovation, an ability to experiment and practise without a concern for the wider or longer-term implications, and without having to expend resources on the agency's survival. However, as the Community Development Foundation's Leominster Marches Project discovered in the early 1980s, a considerable amount of time and energy may have to be devoted to such activities as getting to know the area, getting accepted, and adjusting the project's terms of reference to make them workable. A long-established agency would normally have a head start here.

Permanent agencies/projects and short-life ones each face opportunities and constraints which will influence what is possible in a strategy. This goes beyond simply a question of what can be achieved in the time available. It is to do with the nurturing in communities of long or short time horizons, the degree of acceptable risk-taking and the nature of the relationship between an agency and its constituencies. The fact that they often have complementary advantages means that permanent agencies may need to incorporate short-life projects alongside their longer-term work, and also that there is often room for permanent and short-life community work agencies to work side-by-side in the same locality. In areas with little or no permanent community work resources, a short-life project may be all that is practically possible.

Agency status

In 1983 the majority of community workers (59 per cent) in the UK were employed by voluntary (i.e. non-profit, non-statutory) organisations. In the rural areas of England and Wales, the proportion would probably be at least 95 per cent, but considerably lower in rural Scotland (where the Regional Councils were more significant employers) and in rural Northern Ireland (where there was very little paid rural community work).

During the period of rapid growth in urban community work, debates emerged about the most appropriate agency setting for community work: was it 'better' in a statutory or voluntary organisation; in a social services, education, housing, leisure or planning department of a local authority; in a local or regional/ national agency etc.? We do not wish to repeat these debates, but rather to point to the significance of agency status to a rural community work strategy.

In both Scotland and Northern Ireland, we found that local authority community workers ran into difficulties with their own employers when they attempted to politicise issues. The cultivation of self-help was safe and undemanding, and therefore acceptable. However, the stimulation of demand and protest, which caused difficulty for local authority departments, was not so acceptable, and action was sometimes taken to call the workers to heel.

Community work in a local authority department *can* ensure a direct line to resources and decision-makers, but often community workers are viewed as marginal to the main policy and service parts of the local authority, and so command little influence. On the negative side it may do the worker's own legitimacy and credibility no good to be identified with 'the council': the collectors of local taxes, the takers of unpopular planning decisions, the people who occasionally fail to empty the dustbins, and all the other negative attitudes which people have about local authorities.

In Northern Ireland, some of the district council community workers whom we talked to found that they could work more effectively by being distanced – politically and managerially – from the mainstream core of the local authority. Operating in a quasi-independent way, with groups and on issues which received little overt attention from the politicians, much of their work (around themes of recreation, community/village halls etc) was remarkably similar to that of community workers in English and Welsh rural community councils and Scottish community education departments. Despite possible concerns about political accountability and managerial control, this detached, independent form of action was arguably the only way of effectively operating across the community, where identification with local authority politics would mean the 'sectarianisation' of activities.

Distancing oneself from the local authority which employs you may be pragmatically advisable in building a rapport with constituencies in communities, but it can cause problems. The downside of independence and freedom is a lack of support and of helpful supervision, which should be key elements of a community work 'infrastructure'.

In contrast, a voluntary sector agency base will probably provide a 'user-friendly' image to the constituency: a picture of independent support for voluntary and community action, unsullied by the political expediencies of local authorities. Voluntary agencies such as rural community councils and councils of voluntary service can also demonstrate a degree of community-ownership for, through the membership of their management committees, they can involve representatives of various community networks. However, such agencies can only be as good as their membership, staffing and resources permit. One commentator has observed of RCCs:

> they are, and are likely to remain, poorly equipped to act as very forceful pressure groups on behalf of the rural poor and deprived. They lack the staff and the appropriate structure to become a grass-roots organisation. Since their committees remain the preserve of 'the county great and the good' a paternalistic, consensual approach to rural problems is ensured. In addition, in contrast to the emphasis in urban community development on social welfare, social justice and political definitions of deprivation, RCCs are pervaded by an apolitical ethos of voluntary activity. Finally, the source of their funding is likely to place bounds on the extent to which they could adopt a radical or campaigning role. (Lowe and Buller, 1985)

While we know that there is some truth in this, it is an over-generalisation, and the authors acknowledge that much depends on *who* occupies key positions in the organisation. We also believe that apparently consensual or conservative approaches occur in rural community work not merely because of the status and composition of the agency, but because of the very nature of the communities themselves.

Although the community's perception of the agency is important in determining what can and cannot be done, just as important are the influences which other parts of the agency may bring to bear on the community work strategy. This might be, for example, an expectation to specialise in the main subject area of the host local authority department (such as youth issues in an education department, or welfare rights in a social services department), or to operate particular activities (which may have little community work priority) to satisfy particular funders. All of these pressures may influence the agency's ability to prioritise its action, to choose between generic and specialist approaches to community work, to prioritise groups or areas and to choose the degree of conservatism or radicalism in the strategy.

Available resources

The resources which are available to the agency and worker are crucial to the strategy. Taken in combination with the size and nature of the constituency, the strategy will be heavily constrained or influenced by the resources available: money and staff, skills, access to information, premises, equipment, management and development structures. The aim of the strategy must be to match the work to the resources available.

The resources may be unchangeable, or part of the strategy may be a plan to increase the resources, through fund-raising, staff secondments, use of voluntary labour, networking and co-operation. The strategy must be realistic in terms of resources. In practice we have found that rural community work is already obtaining more from its resources than it can reasonably expect: staff working long hours, generally on low pay. Arguably, a strategy should be wary about taking this level of commitment for granted. It should also build in appropriate rewards and systems of development, not only to improve practice but also to maintain the commitment and enthusiasm of workers.

Staff resources are a question both of quantity and quality. There are relatively few community work staff, and large rural areas to cover. This means that the strategy must either spread the butter thinly, or take hard decisions about prioritising or targetting, or (less realistically) attempt to secure considerably more resources.

The quality of rural community work staff and their agencies seems to us variable. At their best, we found agencies with a well-developed strategy for addressing the needs of their areas. They have an awareness of emerging issues, know their way around the political system and have a system for supporting and enhancing the performance of their staff. The staff themselves have community work skills, and they are adopting a diversity of traditional responsive and innovative approaches to support and develop the communities in their patches. However, not all agencies and workers meet these standards.

The 1983 survey of community workers showed that many of the staff of rural voluntary agencies had little directly relevant training or previous experience, and only stayed in the job for a few years before moving into some quite different line of work. Our knowledge of the field does not suggest that this pattern has changed. A strategy, to be realistic, has to take account of the level of skill, knowledge and personality of each of the workers, as well as their total number.

Money is a key resource, not only because it can determine the number (and to some extent quality) of staff, but also because it can provide other useful tools in the community work strategy, such as the provision of pump-priming grants for community initiatives, or the purchase of equipment such as computers or photocopiers for community use. It is possible to 'stretch' the financial resources through the use of cost-cutting measures, voluntary work, sharing resources with other agencies and numerous other inspired ways.

Apart from other earmarked grants, there is no fixed way of allocating the agency's money to different expenditure headings. It can all be spent on staff, office and travel costs, or some can be spent on grant-aiding communities, or on buying-in specialist consultants, or on paying other agencies to undertake certain tasks. Different combinations are possible, and should be reflected in the strategy. The 'bottom line' of these strategic choices is, as ever, that the strategy must be financially viable.

The nature of the constituency

The nature of the community work agency's constituency should strongly influence the content of the strategy and, to some extent, the strategy can also influence the selection or refinement of the constituency. In Chapter 2, we looked at the common and contrasting characteristics of rural communities in the UK. Being aware of and sensitive to these characteristics is important in developing the community work strategy, although the implementation of the strategy is itself a learning process which will further heighten the worker's and agency's knowledge of the constituency. The strategy cannot be too prescriptive or rigid, because it must allow for the communities themselves to set their own agendas, to identify problems and priorities, and to decide what action to take.

Therefore, in taking account of the nature of the constituency, the challenge for the strategy is to find ways of doing community work which are realistic and appropriate to the constituency. For example, there is little point in putting too much emphasis upon running 'community development through adult education' type classes in a county if local people are not accustomed to attending such classes, and do not like travelling very far out of their own community. Similarly, a strategy which is based on responding to requests for assistance from parish/community councils is little use to communities which either have no parish council at all, or have a council which either lacks the confidence to ask for help, or is too complacent to do so.

Some of the main factors to take account of in 'knowing the constituency' are as follows:

The geography

Frequently, the constituency of a rural community work agency is determined by local government boundaries. The rural areas can be vast, often running into thousands of square miles, and the rural population might be several thousands, or even amount to some hundreds of thousands. Faced with a large array of villages and hamlets, each with their own needs and opportunities, the community worker has to take tough decisions about priorities: whether to try and give *some* sort of support to all of them, or to target resources on to a selected few.

Targetting may be the inevitable result of severely limited resources, but it can also be the deliberate choice of an agency or worker to adopt a punchy, intensive approach, possibly for a short time-span of several years. Focusing a strategy in this way can allow appropriate levels of resources to be brought to bear, and appropriate ways of working to be geared to the locality: see, for example the East Durham 2000 Project (Durham RCC, 1990), the West Glamorgan Valleys Project (West Glamorgan CVS, 1990) and the South Armagh farm diversification project (Rural Action Project, 1989).

The settlement pattern of an area can aid or constrain a community work strategy. Normally, the job is easier in nucleated villages of several hundred or more people, where there is quite likely to be a range of services, focal points, community groups and key individuals, with whom the worker can communicate, and stimulate and support community-based action. The presence of small country towns or larger villages can also be significant: not only as a target for attention in their own right (often, the 'people with problems and needs' have been shifted there from the villages) but also as a central place for carrying out area-wide community work, e.g. running a training workshop for community activists, or establishing a community resource centre.

Climate can also be significant, not only for the more northerly or upland areas where cold winters and snow can deter the running of collective activities outside the home, but also for its effect on seasonal activities. In many areas, rural community work cannot ignore the annual farming cycle, the tourist season and the influence of the climate.

Finally, a large rural constituency has implicatons for resources. Travel costs and travel time will be exceptionally high, requiring special budget provision. This will affect not only the ability of the agency to reach-out to the constituency, but also the extent to which remoter communities will identify and make contact with an agency which is perceived as distant.

The nature of the problems or issues

A community work strategy needs to be flexible and open-minded in order to learn about and adapt to issues and concerns which emerge during the community work process. This does not mean, however, that the strategy can be drawn up in ignorance of problems and issues. There are several reasons for this:

—— Especially in those areas where people may have little concept of community work, the presentation by the worker or agency of knowledge and skill, e.g. of social housing needs or fund-raising, may provide the necessary first link with the community: a point of entry to a much wider range of opportunities.

—— The agency and its workers may already have particular skills, knowledge and interests, and it is important to know whether these are relevant and 'marketable' to the constituency, or whether the strategy needs to help the agency to diversify or re-specialise in order to meet the constituency's real needs.

—— In view of the danger of rural community workers and agencies picking up a biased or partial view of local needs, as expressed by those who shout loudest, the strategy needs to be guided by a wider, more 'objective' assessment of problems and needs, beyond those which are being articulated to the agency by organised community groups.

For these reasons, in planning a rural community work strategy one needs to take account of the problems and issues in the constituency: not only current matters, but also those which are likely to emerge in the foreseeable future. This process calls for a combination of research, monitoring of local and national trends, extrapolation or prediction into the near future, and a certain amount of inspiration and vision as well. Community work needs to be something more than a pragmatic response to the needs of the day.

The communities and people

The question always arises in rural community work, 'how do you take account of the many different and unique communities in developing a community work strategy?' The answer, at the agency level, is that you probably cannot in any great detail. You certainly cannot plan, in a strategic sense, 300 tailor-made responses to 300 different communities. But you do need to be aware of, and sensitive to, this diversity when you put your strategy together.

We can ask ourselves questions such as, 'If we decide to mount an action-research campaign to do something about under-employment and low pay, what kind of response are we likely to get from the sort of village like 'x', where the parish council is always telling us that their only problem is too much new house-building and that people are otherwise content?' Or, 'If we want to concentrate on helping rural women to enhance their social and job-related skills, what do we need to do to get beyond the natural joiners in the Women's Institutes and playgroup committees?'. Thus, at this broad level, even when the strategy is still being devised, some knowledge of the communities and individuals in the constituency is needed in order to select appropriate working methods. These details cannot simply be left to chance.

Existence and potential of other agencies

Even in areas where resources and voluntary and public agencies are thin on the ground, community workers should not act as if they are the sole practitioners of community development. In addition to key individuals within communities who can be encouraged and supported to undertake community work, there is also a range of other agencies and workers who can be drawn in. Some, such as the clergy, may already have a community (if not community development) focus to their work. Others, such as adult education organisers, social workers and citizens advice bureau staff may stand to benefit by adopting a community perspective. They thus represent a resource in the community work strategy, not just another burden-some agency or individual to be worked-around or avoided.

Such people may be resources in more than one way. They may be well placed to work directly with particular communities or with particular issues, possibly bringing new skills, knowledge and working methods to bear. They may be able to offer complementary services, backed up with resources from their own agency. They may be a source of information and insight into areas and communities where one's own agency has had little previous experience, or bring a new perspective to some 'old problems'. Finally, one step back from the operational level, other agencies and other workers can provide an important means of support, ideas and encouragement for the lone rural community worker. The following are some examples:

- In Northern Ireland, we found community workers operating alongside the development officer of a grant-making trust, to bring a variety of community development and project development advice to local people.

- In a remote part of Scotland, we found a close day-to-day partnership between the council of social service, community education workers, and a rural training association, not only to deliver services jointly on the ground but also to provide mutual support and encouragement among the workers.

- In County Durham and Herefordshire, community workers have worked closely with the Workers Education Association to run 'community development through adult education' type courses.

- In Northumberland, the rural community council has devoted time and energy to developing Age Concern, Pre-school Playgroups Association and Citizens' Advice Bureau services to offer specialist help, and to reach more effectively than the RCC could itself, to sections of the RCC's constituency.

- In one part of Scotland, the council of social/voluntary service was working very closely with a local social worker, who saw the CSS as a key mechanism for achieving his own department's community social work aspirations.

- In many local rural community 'patch-work' projects, it is professionals such as the postman, health visitor and GP that the community worker turns to for insight into the lives and needs of individuals, beyond the expressed needs of community groups.

These few cameos show how the existence of other agencies and professionals has a particular significance at the operational level. However, it is important that account is also taken at a more strategic level so that, for example, a community work agency may need to plan to forge closer links with the local youth service, to train and nurture their staff to adopt a wider community focus, and to plan some joint action in a particular locality. Alternatively, where more than one agency is doing generic community work in a particular locality, the agency may need to negotiate some common agreement over demarcation.

Moving from ideas to a strategy

The evolution of a rural community work strategy is more than rigid adherence to a process. It requires appropriate knowledge, skill and values or attitudes. The skills which are required to think and act strategically need to be understood within a framework which involves:

------ looking comprehensively at one's own and one's agency's situation, in relation to the outside world
------ appraising what *should* be done and balancing this with what *can* be done in the light of the resources available and of the constraints and expectations placed on the agency
------ and then mobilising a package of actions concerned directly or indirectly with community work

Implementation itself will need programming, to phase and co-ordinate different pieces of action and to draw in the right resources at the right time. Throughout the implementation, the agency/worker, the constituency and the wider world need to be constantly monitored and the actions evaluated so that, through a process of learning, the strategy can be amended and refined as time goes on. In this way, a strategic approach to practising rural community work is a cyclical or continuous process and not a one-off event with a beginning, middle and end.

The relative shortage of experience of strategic approaches in UK rural community work has meant that we have had little practical material on which to draw. Therefore, in putting forward one possible process for a strategic approach, we recognise that it is not well founded in practical experience nor is it likely to be the only process. We offer it to be tried out in practice, or rejected in an informed and rational way in favour of some preferred approach. The process is based on so-called 'rational approaches' in disciplines such as planning and management:

(i) *Setting overall aims* – based upon an exploration and assessment of values. Here, the decision in rural community work about developmental and functional aims is crucial. Other important value areas include questions of social justice, the role, scope and nature of community-based voluntary action in society, the place of rural areas in our society and economy, and of particular people and groups in communities.

Concern with values may appear as a nebulous beginning to an apparently 'technical' process, but it is fundamental in conditioning every subsequent stage, as well as the resultant strategy. Too often, questions of values are dodged, or glossed over. This results in conflicts and inconsistencies later on when they finally manifest themselves.

(ii) *Identifying and appraising constituencies* – and current and future issues, and their ability to address them without external intervention. This cannot be a penetrating analysis at this stage, but it is necessary at a broad level in order to establish priorities as well as to be prepared for emerging issues and opportunities.

(iii) *Identifying and appraising what others are doing* – in order to identify possible points of conflict and avoid duplication, and more positively to identify scope for collaboration. In the language of the planner, it is the analysis of related decision areas, and at a basic level it means knowing who else is in the same game. It needs to go hand-in-hand with (ii) above.

(iv) *Identifying and appraising your own situation* – for the agency, this will mean looking at its own resources, structures, track record, strengths and weaknesses, quantity and quality of staff, existing commitments. It will also need to take account of its own maintenance/survival/internal development needs, such as public relations, fund-raising, training and staff development and accountability. Many of these issues will also apply to the individual worker.

(v) *Refining your idea of constituency and priorities* – in the light of what seems possible, balancing the work needed with the resources which are or might be available. At this stage, it may be obvious that resource limitations are so severe that any resultant options will be limited, and so it will save time and effort in later stages to begin to limit the constituency, the range of issues, the people and groups, the geographical areas which are likely to figure in the strategy. This process may amount to the setting of goals or targets.

(vi) *Considering and choosing alternative courses of action* – the task at this stage of the process is to consider a wide range of alternatives and to refine and evaluate them against resources, values and aims and against the agency's priorities and objectives.

(vii) *Putting together the strategy* – this is the specification of the package of activities which the agency intends to take, set in the context of resources, values, aims, objectives and priorities as above, and with some indication of their timing or phasing. If it has not happened earlier, this may be an opportune time to consult/ negotiate with other key agencies and the constituency over the content of the strategy.

(viii) *Implementation* – this requires the mobilisation of resources, the detailed operational programming (turning broad ideas into practical plans) and of course the executive action on the ground.

(ix) *Monitoring, evaluating, learning and feeding back* – these are processes which should carry on as the strategy is implemented, and not left as an afterthought when the strategy has been fully implemented. Monitoring is the relatively easy, mechanistic bit. It is effective evaluation, a willingness to learn and to modify the strategy, which provide the greatest challenge.

Practical examples

How might the above process work out in practice? Pressures from central and local government for strategy and evaluation in public sector and publicly funded work are already finding their way through to some areas of rural community work. Thus, in the late 1980s we saw English rural community councils being prompted by their main funders, the Rural Development Commission, into adopting a system of 3-year strategies, annual work programmes, greater accountability, and tighter evaluation. We are likely, there-fore, to see increased pressures on agencies to provide strategic plans for their community work. The following are two examples of agencies which have taken seriously the idea of strategy. They suggest the kind of approach which is being demanded of increas-ing numbers of rural agencies:

The Gordon Rural Advice and Information Network is a council of voluntary service in a remote rural part of Aberdeenshire. Its reports show: active collaboration with various statutory agencies; a portfolio of social welfare, environmental, health, education, employment, information and enterprise work; balance of neighbourhood level and area-wide work; an outreach strategy to extend services from the original office resource base in Huntly; and a programme to secure and retain extra resources.

GRAIN is well known and connected with statutory, voluntary and community networks, and adopts a programmed approach to its work, year by year. This is an example of an agency which does community work, but which also has responsibilities for organising personal social service volunteering and for aspects of social planning. It is typical of many such agencies throughout Britain which have to meet a variety of objectives – of which community development is but one. The challenge, as always, is to find the right balance. (GRAIN, 1989)

The Northern Ireland Rural Action Project is a good illustration of a short-term, 'national' rural community work strategy, which made the most of the limitations of time, few community networks, little previous community work experience in the Province, an under-developed rural policy context and the dangers of a highly charged sectarian environment. The project set out to: identify aspects of rural deprivation; test the delivery of advice and information to rural areas through mobile units; implement an integrated community development approach to revitalise rural communities; and develop statutory–voluntary collaboration in rural areas.

The project progressed through a combination of action and research which focused on four localities: South Armagh (taking action with small farmers and unemployed women); West Fermanagh (working mainly with a locally based generic community development group); Strabane (running a mobile citizens' advice bureau); and the Glens of Antrim (working mainly on tourism issues and on services for elderly people). By devising a range of approaches, in a range of localities, the project made effective use of limited resources. It generated a creditable amount of success on the ground, as well as published material and a stronger lobby to push for more action and better resources for rural community work in the future. (Rural Action Project, 1989)

In this chapter we have sought to argue that every rural community work agency, team or practitioner needs to consider a number of factors when planning a strategy. These range from difficult value questions to those concerned with budgeting and staff training. Almost by definition a strategy has to be 'rounded', to have been built up from several angles and different disciplines. In this way, use of the strategy-building process will avoid any tendency to become mechanistic.

4

A Model of Rural Community Work

Practising community work in rural areas is not wholly different from urban community work; the values underpinning the practice are the same. The crucial point is that the intervention of rural community work is applied in a particular context. The nature of rural communities, and the institutions, agencies and organisations operating in them, demand a relevant, appropriate form of practice, one which differs from the urban experience and is more than a diluted version of it. Difficulties can arise if workers attempt to apply a model which fails to recognise key characteristics of rural life.

In this chapter we describe the main elements of a rural model, and in the following three chapters we go into them in more detail. This way of proceeding will provide a clear pathway for the reader. It also deliberately relates two kinds of theoretical proposition. The first constitutes 'knowledge about' community work – and is reflected in this chapter. It treats community work as an object of study in its own right which has to be explained. The second kind of proposition has to do with practice-theory, 'knowing how' propositions. These are statements, grounded in an analysis of community work experience, which specify the activities and tasks of community work, the role of the worker, the skills needed, and the methods and techniques which can be used. It is crucial to make connections between these two types of theory.

A focus on models is, of course, only one aspect of community work theory. Furthermore, models have limited use. Essentially they offer a way of conceptualising and ordering related ideas. They provide a framework, to an extent artificially separating out different approaches – artificial because in reality the activities are closely interrelated. Thus a community work model exists to guide practitioners and managers – and no more. It does not profess to offer explanations. Too much should not be expected of it.

Working with and for rural communities

There is a widely held belief that community work, to be effective, requires a preoccupation with face-to-face work between the practitioner and local people in communities, over a considerable period of time. This belief is fundamental to most community work teaching and training in the UK and abroad, and is commonly held by urban and rural practitioners alike. The processes, skills, values, knowledge and roles of this type of work are discussed in depth in a variety of texts.

At the heart of this kind of community work – usually termed neighbourhood work – is the proximity, accessibility and availability of the community worker to the people with whom she is working. This closeness is important not only so that her advice, knowledge and expertise is readily and easily available at the moment that the community needs it, but also so that a bond can develop, built upon trust and confidence. This trust is extremely important if the worker is to facilitate the involvement of those who do not readily participate in community activities, and to go beyond the very superficial level of expressed needs and relationships in the community.

The survey of community workers which we carried out (Francis *et al.*, 1984) showed that neighbourhood work, as a form of community work practice, was practised in most British cities, both in the inner areas and the peripheral council housing estates. However, both that survey, and the research which we have undertaken for this book, have shown that neighbourhood work is the exception rather than the norm in almost every rural part of the United Kingdom.

The reasons are not hard to find. In common with most other public resources, the money and people available for community work as a planned activity are much lower (per head of population) than in towns and cities. This may be a reflection both of the reluctance of many public sector agencies in rural areas to spend money on what are often seen as desirable but non-essential activities, and of the higher costs of 'servicing' scattered rural populations.

It is also the case that the geography of rural areas works against neighbourhood work. While this approach is quite realistic in a peripheral urban estate of 5000 people, concentrated within a square kilometre, the focus is lost when in the rural setting the 5000 people may be scattered in villages, hamlets and farmsteads over an area of 1000 square kilometres or more. In rural areas, the community worker's constituency is vast in area and diverse in the range of communities, and often the population numbers are much greater as well. The people with particular needs (arising, for example, from low pay or physical disability) are scattered throughout this constituency and there are likely to be both needs and opportunities in each and every community.

There therefore exists in rural community work a very real dilemma. On the one hand, face-to-face work is seen as the ideal (perhaps the only) form of practice, if community work is to be anything more than a superficial and remote form of servicing for organised community groups. On the other is the realisation that lack of resources and the geographical nature of rural areas make neighbourhood work less realistic, and that the outcome is to spread scarce community work resources very thinly indeed.

The challenge for community work in rural areas is to make the most of what is or could be made available, to make it appropriate to the geographical and social nature of rural communities.

Ways of working

While neighbourhood work – or direct community work, as we propose to call it – is not likely to be a common form of community work practice in rural areas, this does not invalidate it as a way of working. There are examples of good practice in the UK and in other parts of Europe. Some of them spring from the involvement of voluntary (i.e. unpaid) activists from within the community, some result from the interventions of community workers and other professionals.

At the other end of the scale to direct community work is the much more common rural community work practice which has no particular title, but which we shall describe as 'working from a distance'. It is typified by the county-wide approach of rural community councils and councils of voluntary service in England, Wales and Scotland, community education workers in Scotland, and community services officers in Northern Ireland. It places a greater emphasis on working *for* a number of communities, and less on working *with* them. Contact with communities is likely to be via such media as the telephone, the postal services, newsletters and (increasingly in the 1990s) computers rather than through face-to-face work.

'Working from a distance' accepts that the outcome, from a community work point of view, may not be as effective as direct work, but hard choices have to be made between concentrating one's resources for the full benefit of one or a few communities, or spreading these resources for a lesser (but nevertheless tangible) benefit of all or most communities. Maximising the spread of these resources, by working even-handedly with the whole of the constituency, may be viewed as making the most efficient use of them, because the maximum number of communities can be helped.

To an extent, the 'direct work' versus 'working from a distance' choice could be seen as a choice between effectiveness and efficiency, or between quality and quantity. We would dispute this over-simplification, because we believe that quality and effectiveness can still be achieved through working from a distance, and that it is also possible to be efficient and to spread the benefits when practising direct community work.

Furthermore, we do not see there being a simple choice between two extremes. Our conceptualisation of community work allows for at least a third choice. This can be viewed either as the introduction of a focus to working from a distance, or as a broadening-out of direct work. We call this approach 'focused, indirect work'.

Three approaches

We have thus identified three approaches to the practice of community work in rural areas. We call this a model, and we see the model as the basis on which practitioners and their agencies can build a strategy. We do not claim it to be uniquely rural. Nor does it stand wholly separate from urban practice. But it does have a special relevance in rural areas, due to the combination of scarce resources and scatter of rural communities. It is designed specifically for the rural community worker and for other rural practitioners and their agencies.

The usefulness of the model will lie in helping workers and their agencies to make rational, informed choices about how to deploy very limited resources. Each of the three strands provides a framework within which to practice community work. One or other of the strands will be more appropriate to some agencies than others; for example, a village-based community association is most likely to function within the direct community work part of the model.

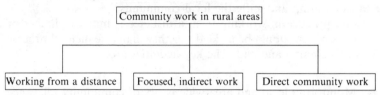

However, we are not wishing to enforce the allocation of just one of the three strands to a worker or agency. Rather, we are looking to agencies and workers both to *move between* different parts of the model over time, and to *combine* different parts at the same time. In this way the benefits of the model, in terms of a more rational, sharper approach to rural community work, are obtained, but not at the expense of maximising the possibilities of a worker or project. On the contrary, the model should lead to greater sophistication in planning, practising and evaluating rural community work.

Working from a distance

Working from a distance is a form of community work practice which makes sense of the mismatch between the small number of community work resources and the large number of communities which could benefit. It does this by aiming to maximise the spread of resources in the most effective manner possible. It recognises that all communities have needs, and that the agency and/or worker has a duty to help all of them at some point. It is especially suited to the aim of helping rural communities to survive, against the pressures of rural decline, increasing public apathy and centralisation of power. However, it is not purely defensive. Working from a distance also enables communities to flourish and develop, although this requires a high level of motivation and ability within the community, and the opportunity for the community worker to influence how this process takes place is limited.

Its advantages are in its efficient distribution of community work resources. Because no community can grab the lion's share of attention, it avoids the risk of creating a strong dependency relationship which can leave a community vulnerable and (in some respects) weak if and when the worker finally withdraws. For the same reason, it also avoids the risk of 'overkill': of so much attention and community work resources being concentrated on a small area or group that it is wasteful of community work resources and can swamp and stifle the local community.

Good practice in working from a distance is more a number of activities which should be tackled together than a sequential process with a beginning and end. The key activities are:

- Monitoring local and area-wide issues of community relevance or interest.
- Researching issues.
- Working to influence other agencies.
- Advising and informing communities.
- Supporting and developing networks of community groups.

It follows from the approach of working from a distance that there may be little face-to-face contact with people in their own communities. There will certainly be contact via the telephone, correspondence and computer interaction, and contact with those people who come from local communities to area-wide conferences, training days and county committee meetings. Statements and other indicators which the worker receives about each community may have to be taken at face value, or subject only to a limited amount of checking or corroboration, because she does not have much time or means of doing more than this.

Arguably, only a relatively limited understanding of the community is possible, or even necessary, as the worker fulfils the role of the outside, and distanced, expert: advising on grant aid schemes, giving information about committee procedures and constitutions, advising groups on who in the local council should be lobbied about a particular problem.

Linked with this is the low frequency of contact. Apart from sending out a regular newsletter and briefing sheets, it may be quite common for a community work agency to be in touch with a particular community over a particular issue only once every three or four years. With the turnover of workers which is common in many agencies, a community worker may therefore come into contact with a community once, and then only with a single individual from that community, and only for a single issue or project.

These constraints cut against the notion of the community worker knowing the patch and the people well (and vice-versa), with a richness of understanding and warmth built up over a period of time. It calls for a special range of skills and knowledge and an attitude of mind. It is an approach which largely has to accept the nature of rural communities, and help them to achieve whatever they identify as priorities. Almost invariably these tend to be concerned more with the tangible ends of community work (community buildings, care schemes, schools saved from closure, etc.) than with the less tangible ends of human relationships: social equality, learning through participating, mutual support.

Working from a distance is largely based upon consensus and co-operation, partly because of its philosophy of linking together the scarce resources in a variety of agencies, institutions and groups to help them all pull in the same direction, and partly because (as we have discussed in earlier chapters) this is likely to be the natural face of rural life as presented to 'outside' community workers. This does not mean that campaigning and other lobbying cannot happen, but it is likely to be within a broadly consensual framework.

Working from a distance, if done effectively, can provide a passable level of support for the majority of rural communities. However, it can take its toll in low worker morale: you never get to know any community well, or see a project through from start to finish, and you are never quite sure how much of a community's 'success' was due to your own contribution. By making the best of a poor (under-resourced) job, it also runs the risk of reinforcing the status quo of under-resourcing and of existing power structures and patterns of disadvantage.

Focused, indirect work

Focused indirect work is a form of community work whereby the practitioner engages with a limited number of communities, and people within communities, on a number of issues and over a period of time. It is, in effect, a balanced compromise between the efficiency of working from a distance and the effectiveness of direct community work. Typically it is a strategy which comes about from an area-wide agency or worker deciding to target a particular area, or type of community, but it can also represent an extending-out of a direct community work approach into a wider area.

This approach is based on a conscious decision not to spread scarce resources thinly, all at the same time, but to focus them sufficiently to be more effective. It is a way of overcoming some of the difficulties of working in rural communities: the geographical and psychological distance of the agency from the periphery, the constraints of power bases in communities, the lure of purely tangible outcomes. However, the community work resources are still finite, so hard decisions must be made about priorities.

The main activities of focused, indirect work include:

● Targetting particular communities.
● Creating opportunities to work with particular communities or groups.
● Working with and beyond key actors.
● Broadening people's agendas.
● Effective withdrawal.

Although the above are the key areas of involvement by the worker within targetted communities, other essential activities need to be sustained outside the community. The worker's or agency's wider constituency, which may have been given a lower or a future priority, will still need to be sustained, involving many of the techniques in working from a distance. At the same time, there is a continuing need to keep abreast of wider issues, trends, opportunities and resources. Some of this may be of benefit to the targetted communities, and some to the worker's or agency's wider constituency, or to her own practice.

The advantages of focused, indirect work are that it allows a certain amount of in-depth, effective work with particular communities, while still not neglecting the majority. Through it, communities can be more ambitious, disadvantaged people can achieve greater power and responsibility, and greater attention can be given to processes and relationships, not just to tangible end results. By close personal involvement over a period of time, there should also be greater worker satisfaction.

On the other hand, the difficulty of finding acceptable and reliable criteria for targetting can lead to inappropriate focusing. The preoccupation with targetting can mean that resources and initiatives might be imposed on communities who do not want them, or who grab them without taking account of the consequences. Because resources are limited, the imposition of a programmed approach can lead to compromises, especially in condensing the beginnings and endings of involvement with a particular community, and an overall danger that the community is being slotted into the agency's own agenda and timetable, when the reverse is preferable.

Nevertheless, focused indirect work constitutes a crucial opportunity for the resource-efficient agency and worker to spend at least some of their time and effort in a more effective, targetted way.

Direct community work

Neighbourhood work is the classic approach to community work which involves a close and protracted working relationship between the worker and the community. It has been analysed and elucidated by Henderson and Thomas (1987) and others.

In rural areas, availability of the worker doing direct community work allows her to be involved in all parts of the community work process. She can relate to a large number of groups and individuals in the community, and be part of and influence the life of the community. Direct community work gives the worker a very real stake in the processes and outcomes.

The main activities of direct community work are:

● Building trust, confidence and relationships with and between all parts of the community.
● Strengthening and building groups.
● Facilitating the creation of a strategy.
● Putting ideas into action.
● Refreshment and regeneration.

Direct community work requires the worker to become immersed in the community. It is simply not possible to stay detached. This places demands on both the 'professional' and the private life of the worker, with implications for the worker's objectivity, sense of perspective, privacy and allegiance. In a rural area, the community worker who is employed by an agency may well be operating at considerable distance from the agency's base, with little day-to-day support or supervision, or contact with peers. The tendency to become an integral part of the community, experiencing and sharing its values, can be overwhelming. This has both advantages and dangers. For the voluntary activist in particular, direct community work can be a personally rewarding and highly effective means of facilitating community work, but it can result in isolation, and in the individual's credibility and legitimacy being challenged by some local people.

In describing the essence of the three approaches to rural community work we have moved from identifying them at a theoretical level (models) to perceiving them as the basis of a rational decision-making process (strategy). We now take further the refining and specifying of how the work is to be done.

5

Working from a Distance

In putting forward the idea that working from a distance constitutes a major plank of rural community work strategy, we are aware that we tread on thin ice. Some experienced practitioners in particular have alerted us to the danger of treating rural communities very superficially. Arguably many people in rural areas are more curious about outsiders than their urban counterparts, not simply in the sense of knowing who someone is but also because they wish to understand him or her. Thus for rural agencies to stand off, as it were, from rural communities risks missing the point.

The counter-argument is threefold. Firstly, working from a distance is a rational response to the widespread needs of the community work agency's area, where the agency is faced with the reality of the very low level of resources available to support rural community action. Deciding to 'spread the jam thinly' is tough-minded and risky because the resources may be too dispersed to be effective, but it is a realistic option in that it has the potential to give something to all communities in the agency's area.

Secondly, we believe that it *is* possible for staff, in working from a distance, to respect the ways in which rural people think and behave. Approaches to communities *must* be rooted in a sound understanding of them, in ways we outlined in Chapter 2. Accordingly, as we shall see, working from a distance requires a high level of skills in a number of complementary areas. It calls for the worker to operate with considerable professional and political sophistication. He or she has to avoid any suggestion that the approach rides roughshod over the concerns and practices of local people.

Finally, we would argue that in most situations where agencies and staff are working from a distance there should be other supportive activities taking place. These might be from the same agency, or from one or more different organisations, and ideally should complement the work being undertaken from a distance. For example, a health visitor may be supporting a village playgroup, visiting it on a weekly basis, at the same time that an external agency – the Rural Community Council or Social Services Department – keeps in contact only through an occasional newsletter, supplemented by even less frequent direct contact with the playgroup leader. A high level of complementarity is possible, with the health visitor addressing a variety of needs to do with child development, parental concerns, social relationships etc., and the external agency giving advice on, for example, fund-raising for new equipment, influencing local education authority policies on nursery education or whatever other issues periodically crop up.

The benefits arising as a result of working from a distance can be summarised as follows:

—— it helps as many communities as possible, but the nature of the help tends to be general rather than specific
—— it is concerned more with working *for* than *with* each community
—— it is effective when community groups are already basically competent and confident
—— it provides the agency and worker with a wide range of experience of issues and activities, but little experience with the processes
—— it is probably more effective in achieving functional goals (new jobs, village halls, etc.) than developmental ones (a fairer society, a more caring community, etc.)

The implication is that working from a distance is a compromise, but not a perfect one. It achieves results where the factors are already somewhat favourable, but the results which it can achieve are limited, and especially so if a community is not competent and confident to respond to the resources offered by a working from a distance approach.

Process

It is difficult to describe the activities involved in working from a distance as a process, because we see them as being concurrent. They need to proceed in parallel. Of course, in the early part of an agency's existence or of a community worker's posting, there may be a greater emphasis on information-collection activities (getting to know the area) and generally on establishing links and credibility with agencies and networks, but this is only an introductory stage which could be expected in any kind of agency or work situation, unrelated to community work. Once the agency or worker is established, these activities must all proceed together and, while the emphasis on each may vary from time to time, none are dispensable.

We can illustrate the process by reference to the work done by project officers in some of the Rural Development Areas funded by the Rural Development Commission. The worker in the Pennine RDA, for example, concentrated on supporting a number of groups from a strong information and policy base. The RDA spans over 100 square miles between Manchester and the industrial towns and cities of West Yorkshire. Most of the inhabitants live in the towns and villages lining three valleys, and links between them are few (Pennine RDA Strategy Committee, 1988). The worker saw her main role as keeping the rural development programme under review and trying to encourage the two local authorities involved to develop closer partnerships with rural communities. She was aware that she 'walked a tightrope' between being seen as a remote local authority officer and being 'trusted' by local people.

The point is that the RDA worker was valuable to local leaders because she had a strong grasp of the policy issues which have an impact on communities; she kept people informed and met with them from time to time. Equally, she channelled information and brought influence to bear in the policy arenas of key agencies because she was in contact with localities.

In order to operate in the way described above, and to ensure it continues if the key worker leaves, it is essential that the process of working from a distance is clear to those involved. The stages need to be thought through. We identify them as follows:

(i) *Assess the coverage* – this may be an entire county, or some other administrative division. Having decided on the extent of the geographical coverage, the agency or worker has to select and then 'map' the sorts of groups and individuals with or for whom the work will take place. For example, many English rural community councils and Welsh voluntary service councils have chosen to focus a lot of their attention on parish/community councils and village hall committees, and on local influential professionals such as doctors and clergy.

(ii) *Deciding the activities* – the agency or worker must begin activities which are appropriate to the constituency and which are based upon available resources. For example, many agencies have found it resource-efficient and reasonably effective to publish and circulate a newsletter, but few spend a great deal of time undertaking research, because despite its desirability it can be costly and time-consuming.

(iii) *Developing skills and knowledge* – the agency and its workers must establish and maintain a range of skills and information/intelligence necessary to carry out the work. The requirements are diverse: for example, skills such as report-writing, public speaking, data analysis, time management; and knowledge such as new legal requirements, grant aid policies, unemployment trends and political structures.

(iv) *Linking in to other systems* – good connections are needed with other agencies for various reasons: to influence their policies and practice, to make use of their resources, to agree suitable roles, to maximise the opportunities. This requires forging links not only with other agencies in the area but also with agencies operating at a higher level – including those which provide key resources such as support, training and intelligence.

(v) *Implementing the work* – the tasks undertaken by the community worker (see below).

(vi) *Evaluation and reflection* – this is essential if working from a distance is to remain relevant and accessible (see Chapter 8).

Activities

The main elements or activities involved in working from a distance are as follows:

(i) *Monitoring local and area-wide issues of community relevance or interest.* Working from a distance requires the agency and worker to keep abreast of issues for a variety of reasons:

———   to be alert to outside forces which might affect the local area, or the operation of the agency

———   to give a wider and possibly more representative context to the issues being articulated by local groups and leaders

———   to broaden the range of opportunities and resources which the agency and communities can then draw upon

The range of relevant topics is enormous: trends in service and employment provision; the decisions of local authorities, central government and many other agencies: who is doing what, and to whom, in the area; new criteria for grant aid schemes; sources of specialist expertise; the activities of individual communities; good ideas for meeting local needs.

In addition to the range of topics, the material can come from a variety of media: national and international journals, government reports, minutes of council meetings, TV and radio reports, newspaper articles, conversations with other practitioners and community leaders, reports of projects. These sources stand in contrast to the community work practice carried out at a more intimate and local level where a greater amount of information on issues can come from the community itself.

A key skill for the worker is to be able to seek out new sources of information, prioritise what is available, selectively scan it, record it, store it in an ordered way and retrieve it as necessary. This requires of the community worker many of the skills usually associated with administration, but not in any static or stolid way. In addition to office skills, this work also requires imagination and lateral thinking: not only to retain a sense of perspective and to see the wood for the trees, but also to interpret general or peripheral information to make it relevant to the situation of communities and the rurality of the local area.

(ii) *Researching issues.* Undertaking research is, in effect, an extension of the monitoring process, but we identify it as a separate heading because it demands extra skills and generally more resources of time and effort. It is important where sources of information and understanding are unavailable, or where an alternative perspective to the 'conventional wisdom' is required.

One example was the establishment by Avon Community Council of a rural health project designed to build up a comprehensive record of the patterns and coverage of primary health care facilities in rural Avon as perceived by the providers (Payne and Townsend, 1990). From the results, it planned to prepare an information directory for distribution to every household. This illustrates the potential of research to challenge cosy views about rural needs.

Some rural agencies have developed a strong competence in undertaking quick, cheap pieces of research: investigation, for example, into local authority grant aid schemes, or analysis of the likely effects of new VAT provisions on the running costs of village halls and community centres. It was also noticeable that some agencies were alert to research findings emerging from academic and research bodies. For example, Dyfed Association of Voluntary Services made use of a study of population changes and current attitudes in rural Wales (Institute of Welsh Affairs, 1988). In Scotland, the research outputs of the Arkleton Trust are used by a number of rural agencies to develop their strategies.

Community workers have a special interest in knowing about the world as seen by the community, rather than the way policy-makers think they see it. The material may include facts and opinions. They may use primary sources of information (e.g. from their own postal questionnaires) or second-hand sources (such as re-analysing and interpreting official data, which may have been collected for some other purpose). Considerable skill is required, both to choose and to use the appropriate techniques, and to manage the whole operation so that it does not change from being a tool to being an end in its own right.

The number of research subjects is potentially large, and the community worker needs to exercise selectivity and self-control, to ensure that the material is useful and action-orientated. There is plenty of scope for opportunism: for example, arranging with another agency to include questions of interest to you in their questionnaire, or encouraging a local university to undertake research on your behalf. An interesting example of this comes from Wales, where one of the mid-Wales university colleges has undertaken the computer-based analysis of questionnaires produced by community-based village appraisals. The community workers and villages had their analysis done by experts, and the academics also benefited through the expanding database which they built up.

Finally, the worker or agency needs to think through the role of communities – their constituency – in this research. Frequently, local people will be asked to provide the information: for example, a parish council clerk or Women's Institute secretary completing a questionnaire on the range and changes in shops, pubs, schools and other services in the locality. If the 'output' of the research is to be understandable and available to local groups – and we believe it generally should be – this requirement needs to be planned for, to determine not only what the output should be like (in layman's language, not heavy and turgid, etc.), but also how it should be disseminated. The research undertaken by Duncan Scott and colleagues (1991) in the Peak National Park is an excellent example of planned feedback to participants with the aim of supporting action.

The skill of research therefore needs to be accompanied by the art of communication, to ensure not only that there is a message, but also that it is put across effectively and understood.

(iii) *Working to influence other agencies.* In an ideal world, the community worker encourages communities and groups to articulate their own needs and to influence relevant decision-makers and resource-providers. However, the practicalities of a large constituency – and, at times, insufficient time to mobilise a campaign – often require community workers to engage with the agencies directly, on behalf of local communities. The worker or agency is called upon to act as advocate.

National voluntary agencies such as Rural Voice, Rural Forum and the Northern Ireland Rural Association have increasingly put across a general 'rural viewpoint' to government departments and service-providers: often showing how general or city-biased national policies can have unintended effects in rural areas, and educating policy-makers about the special nature of rurality. This role is not confined to national agencies and central government. Especially since the 1970s, English and Welsh RCCs have actively worked to influence the decisions of council departments, public transport operators, oil companies, retailing chains, breweries and public utility suppliers on behalf of local rural communities.

This demands a range of attributes in the worker and agency: a sound knowledge base about the issue in question; legitimacy and credibility with both the constituency and the body being influenced; skills of negotiation, presentation and persuasion; and a sense of realism. It puts a large strain on individual workers and agencies: by expecting them to be specialist experts as well as generalists; by demanding both the balanced overview of the policy-maker, but also the parochial view of the local resident; by pitting one's own role against that of the local elected politician or trained professional; and by attempting to speak for a constituency where there may not be a full consensus on any issue. In a complex world in which the worker's ally over one issue may be their adversary over another, it also calls for a high degree of political sophistication: an ability to cope with ambiguity and contradiction.

Working from a distance will require the practitioner to work through ascribed local leaders: chairperson of a parish council, a vicar, playgroup organiser or simply a longstanding resident. Inevitably, such people can be unrepresentative, or out of touch with feelings and undercurrents in a community, and it is essential for the worker concerned to be alert to this possibility and, if necessary, invest time in making contact with other opinion leaders. Martinez-Brawley (1986), in her study of community-oriented social work on two islands in the Outer Hebrides, picked up the danger when referring to the Council of Social Services:

> The CSS appeared to have focused intensely on enhancing its local legitimacy and has involved a cadre of local leaders. The priest commented that the cadre of local leaders was somewhat narrow.

Effectiveness depends heavily on the capacity of those involved to maintain a sound knowledge base on a number of wide-ranging subjects and issues. Only then will community work from a distance be able to continue to provide useful information to individuals and groups and, vice versa, be in a position to make the connections between practice and policy.

In addition to the monitoring and research functions which provide much of the material for this work, further techniques and areas of understanding are required. Communication is all-important: writing effective letters and reports; getting the most out of face-to-face meetings and committees, using the telephone as a vehicle for negotiation and not just for information. Understanding and knowing one's way around the system is also crucial: who are the decision-makers, the powers behind the thrones, the opinion formers? How are decisions made, and how can they be influenced? When is the best time to make the approach, and with what preparation?

There is a special rural dimension when utilising these broadly 'political' skills, and workers and agencies from an urban background need to adapt to it. We have covered this ground in Chapters 1 and 2, where we talk about conservatism, slow adjustment to change, political independence, individuality, the recurrence of key actors in different roles or settings. Not only may the culture of a rural community be very different from that of the agencies and departments, but there will also be considerable differences within it, particularly between the 'haves' and 'have-nots'.

The rural agency will usually have to relate to several such constituencies – which sometimes include members of its own committee – and it is essential that staff are adept at doing so. There is little scope for a too 'purist' approach by community workers given the political 'map' of most rural areas. This lesson is captured in a case study describing the setting-up of a community-based company in the village of Berinsfield, Oxfordshire. The workers were mostly doing direct community work. However, they were obliged to negotiate at a diocesan and county level. They concluded that:

> it is unprofessional for community workers to live in a fantasy land and confuse political rhetoric with organisational reality. We required a coalition to have any chance of even joining battle let alone winning it. (Bryant and Butcher, undated).

Political skills will certainly need to include the ability to move between, and negotiate with, different interests and factions. This feature is brought out in the description of a community social work team in the Highland Region (Green, 1989). In addition, political skills will often require the ability to encourage conciliation, a recognition that people with differing outlooks and origins have to learn to live together. The involvement of some leaders of the 'Welsh rural agencies, 'PONT' (Bridge), a movement which seeks to make links between indigenous Welsh people and newcomers, is a good example of using such political skills.

(iv) *Advising and informing communities.* This is the function of working from a distance which comes closest to urban community work, and to the two other approaches of focused indirect work and direct work. However, it has a place within this approach where it is at arm's length or sporadic in nature.

In a typically large rural area, the needs of the communities will be immensely varied, as will their need for a community worker. The challenge for the worker and agency is to find an acceptable balance between putting out generalised information 'on spec' to the constituency as a whole, and saving some time and energy to respond to the specific needs of individual communities. There is a narrow divide between comprehensiveness and bland generalisation, and also between an agency which is accessible to all-comers, and one which muddles through with little to offer of substance to any in its constituency.

The skill is to keep a finger on the pulses of both the constituency and the outside world: to feel instinctively, as much as by 'market research', what people need and want to know; to work, at times, beyond the face value of what a group says it wants, to find what it really needs; to provide material which informs, but which also challenges and stretches communities to achieve more. The approach is essentially about demystifying systems, publicising opportunities and constraints, providing a bridge between communities and professionals or bureaucrats.

Isolated villages and settlements frequently have very poor access to sources of information, whether it be about benefits entitlement, planning rules or availability of health and welfare services: 'It is ironic that not only are services a long way off if you live in a rural area, but sources of information about services are often equally distant' (Armstrong and Thompson, 1986). In addition, rural areas are more often than not in the position of having to convince resource-holders that poverty and other problems exist and that people need information and advice in order to respond to them. NCVO's Rural Unit has pursued this theme vigorously in the context of Community Care (see Young, 1990).

It is not just a matter of what the agency does, but also the way in which it does it. For example, a variety of community workers in all parts of the UK provide general information and specific advice to village hall committees, both on the development of new provision, and on day-to-day aspects of running a hall. Most of these workers, we have found, provide a basic range of material: on sources of grant aid, constitutions, licensing requirements, taxation etc. This enables new and existing hall committees to function. However, it takes special skill and inspiration to go beyond this: to change the committees from administrators of premises to active community groups; to help them deal more creatively with new needs; to provide further useful facilities and draw in fresh income.

There is a double challenge to the community worker and agency if they are to be effective in working from a distance: not only must they know their constituency, but they must also be known by it. Because the worker will rarely be present within any community or locality, other ways have to be found of raising one's profile if communities are to be made aware of what is available, so that they can make demands. Therefore, a key part of the process of advising and informing communities is to advertise what is on offer: not only to those groups with whom there is already sufficient contact, but also to those who may have at best only a vague notion about what the agency and worker – and community work as an intervention – can offer. The implication of this is that advising and informing communities requires not only the knowledge and skills for directly performing these tasks; it also requires what can broadly be described as public relations skills. The message itself is important, but so also is the way in which it is made available and delivered.

Therefore specialist knowledge on matters such as grant aid schemes, youth development, welfare rights, town and country planning, which agencies and workers may need to have, must be backed up by presentational processes and skills: the publication of accessible and readable newsletters, briefings and reports; the staging of conferences and training events; the gaining of effective coverage in local newspapers, radio and TV.

Contact with communities is primarily at arm's length, calling for full use of the telephone and letter-writing, and making effective use of the limited amount of direct contact with a local group which occurs when the worker attends its committee meeting. The worker's remoteness means that she or he may not readily be called upon at all stages when help is required. This, combined with the slow pace at which many rural community groups work, means that it may take months or years for a community to work through a particular issue or project, which in turn requires appropriate action by the worker and agency: good record-keeping (which may be important to show the history of a community issue, and the agency's involvement in it) and a follow-up mechanism (to prompt a community group if no progress or contact appears to have been made for some time) are particularly important.

(v) *Supporting and developing networks of community groups.* A key function of community work is to promote collective action to address common needs. Although this generally means bringing individuals together within a community, the practice of working from a distance also operates at the level of bringing together community groups with a common interest over a wider area. This process has validity in any geographical context, but it is especially relevant in rural areas, both to overcome the inherent difficulties of isolation and parochialism of rural communities, and to achieve 'economies of scale' in the contact between an agency and its constituency. By supporting a network (such as pre-school playgroups, youth clubs or a county federation of Young Farmers Clubs), the rural community worker can build upon linkages and energy to achieve wider goals beyond the immediate aims of a group.

In considering this type of work, the agency and worker are faced with the same sort of decisions which face workers at a community level: whether to work through and develop existing networks, or create something entirely new; how to balance the day-to-day servicing of the network (which may be necessary for its continued functioning) with the sort of development work which enables it to achieve wider community objectives; how to manage the level and nature of the agency's involvement and input, so that it does not become a long-term dependent liability, distracting the agency from its own priorities. Inevitably, compromises need to be made between these competing requirements.

In England and Wales, a long-established relationship has developed between the county-wide rural community councils and the county associations of local (i.e. parish-level) councils, in which the RCCs have provided a secretariat and development service for the associations and their member councils. In Scotland, there is a similar relationship between the community education services of the regional or island local authorities, and the local youth councils and adult education associations.

These arrangements have worked best where there has been an interdependence and a sharing of benefits: the community networks benefit from the specialist inputs of community workers, which the networks themselves could not provide for themselves, and in turn the networks provide for a privileged access for the community workers to the groups in the networks, which would not otherwise occur. The arrangements have worked least well when the resource of the community worker has become bogged down in the servicing of the network's formal structure, or in becoming preoccupied only with the mundane procedural and administrative matters of member groups. The skill of networking lies in identifying and making appropriate connections between people involved in similar kinds of work taking place across a wide area.

As with all the activities involved in working from a distance, there are limits to how much networking is possible. Some prioritising is called for, based perhaps on the character of the groups and the ability of different networks to support themselves in due course. The support and development of networks implies a higher level of commitment than is required for other activities involved in working from a distance. It is possible, for example, to reduce or increase the amount of attention given to monitoring, research and lobbying, but the work which is undertaken for a network and its members creates demands and obligations in the fulfilment of which the community work agency usually has less room for manoeuvre.

Role

The practitioner's role when working from a distance can be compared to the positional play of a sweeper on the football field

– covering a wide area, being alert to new initiatives, picking up on issues. Yet it is often a discrete role, because the worker is not operating at the front line. He or she is very much acting as a back-up person, providing – as we have seen – appropriate information, services and support. It is a role familiar to many RCC staff but one that can be played too by staff of other voluntary organisations as well as statutory agencies. In social services departments, for example, a community social worker or community liaison officer can decide to spend a high proportion of his or her time in this role. Within a framework of this sweeper role we would identify the following:

(i) *Analyst*. Here the worker is cast in a role which overlaps those of researcher and political scientist. It is the role where providing a quick, accurate overview of an area is second nature to the person concerned. It is about monitoring developments affecting a county or large rural area, storing, organising and disseminating the data in useful, accessible ways to local contacts and organisations.

More politically, it requires the worker to interpret new developments, to keep close to impending policy changes in powerful agencies and to understand the ebb and flow of ideas and fashion among key officers and elected members. In this sense the analyst is making connections all the time at a policy level, and considering how they relate to resources. She does this on behalf of her agency, which in turn is linked to a rural constituency of some kind.

(ii) *Educator*. In a sense, the practitioner who works from a distance is highly dependent on community leaders and volunteers for her effectiveness. She is working with and through such people to achieve community work objectives. For this reason, it is essential for the worker to support local people, and sometimes this should take the form of education and training. The manager who is supporting area-based staff will need to play a similar role.

It is important to understand the term 'educator' flexibly. Only rarely would the community worker be involved as a tutor on formal training courses. More likely, she would identify particular learning needs of volunteers, local leaders or staff and arrange, and prepare for, a number of informal sessions. For more substantial training requirements, the worker would help to identify appropriate courses.

(iii) *Advocate*. The role of advocate is one of four identified by Spergel (1969) and the term partly fits the rural community worker practising from a distance:

He performs a vigorous mediating or ombudsman function on behalf of dispossessed groups... in their relations with public and voluntary bureaucracies as well as with political structures... He is more interested in the achievement of specific ends than the facilitation of a group process of social development.

The rural community worker may be advocating on behalf of a particular village, or she may be advancing arguments for rural community work in general. Whichever it is, she is setting out to make a case, and needs to have assembled the arguments, and anticipated objections, very carefully. This is clearly especially important when the community worker is seen to take the side of the community against 'authority'. The importance of thinking and acting politically is at a premium here. There is a need to be open and honest with the community group being supported, and astute and articulate with the powerholders.

We emphasise that anyone playing the advocacy role will be obliged to work across several social classes, not assume that she can function or be convincing by only relating to one class or constituency. We think this role, of operating in several 'arenas', contrasts with the community worker's role as normally understood in the context of urban neighbourhood work. There, the community worker will usually have a strong and instinctive rapport with a predominantly working-class constituency and would not expect to have to work also with middle-class groups or networks, except in so far as these are represented on management and other commit-tees. Most rural community work is not like that, and nowhere more so than when work is being done from a distance. The practitioner has to engage with most, if not all, parts of the class system. In the rural setting, if the worker does not adapt the role to a broad social base, she is likely to remain ineffective.

Concluding remarks

Compared with the more face-to-face forms of rural community work discussed in the next two chapters, working from a distance might be seen as a detached experience. The danger of this perception of the practice is that it might be seen as bureaucratic, safe, and an easy option for agencies and workers reluctant to 'dirty their boots' with 'proper' community work. While it is true that working from a distance requires organisation and a range of office-related skills, it would be wrong to dismiss it as a soft option, or as one which is not really community work.

Firstly, it is a high-risk option, because the small amount of direct contact with communities on the ground can mean that at best only a limited range of options are presented to a narrow section of the community, and at worst this practice can miss the mark altogether. Secondly, it is not safe and easy in terms of the skills, knowledge and other resources required. 'Hard' skills such as research, report-writing and keeping abreast of technical issues need to be accompanied by 'softer' skills such as the handling of interpersonal relationships, and being sensitive to local needs and cultures. Being detached from most of the communities in one's constituency does not let workers off the hook of knowing and understanding them: on the contrary, it requires extra skills in piecing together the jigsaw from scraps of information, in combining imagination with hard facts, and in constantly inspiring and innovating to ensure that remoteness does not mean insensitivity or intolerance.

Thirdly, working from a distance presents a major challenge to the worker and agency in managing the work. It is easy for this practice to slip into an exercise in muddling-through: of sitting back and waiting for communities to come to you, then deciding how best to respond to them individually. Good management is necessary not only to prioritise the work and the issues and groups in the constituency, but also to sustain worker effectiveness and morale. Achievements on the ground are hard to identify and measure, and this form of practice needs care and support if conscientious and self-critical workers are not to sink into despair about their effectiveness and worth.

Lastly, working from a distance is a changing, progressive form of practice, with a dynamic derived both from planned changes and opportunities. It can adapt to changes in the agency, the constituency and the wider world. Although it is arguably the longest-established of the three strands of rural community work which we have identified, there is room for refinement and improvement. And we emphasise that it should not be seen as a strategy in its own right: it is one form of rural community work practice, which should be set alongside the other two more direct forms in ways which allow them to support and influence each other.

6

Focused, Indirect Work

The two key ingredients of focused, indirect work are that the choice of where to work is made on the basis of a rational decision-making process and that the intervention is time-limited. The decision-making process does not necessarily have to be sophisticated. Indeed, we found that some fieldworkers had developed the approach as a natural part of good practice. A community care worker in Sussex, for example, had sought to identify the gaps in community care in six parishes. She had visited all the local organisations, in addition to professional staff such as health visitors and teachers, churches and pubs, and as a result of this survey had concentrated her work in particular parts of the patch.

Many rural agencies have developed a focused, indirect approach over a period of time. The basis of the Community Council of Northumberland's strategy, for example, is that, 'We do not have sufficient staff to work *in depth* with all of the communities in Northumberland, and so have evolved an approach and set of priorities to make the most of what we do' (Community Council of Northumberland, 1990). The resulting strategy includes a combination of county-wide responsive services which are available to a wide range of community groups, and some interventions which are specifically targetted on particular issues (e.g. low-cost rentable housing), areas (e.g. the old coalfield, where there is high unemployment and other problems) and types of groups (e.g. parish councils and village hall committees).

A similar capacity to tailor resources is in evidence among some rural service delivery agencies. The southern district of Norfolk's Social Services Department, for example, has evolved a patch-based approach, with a strong inter-agency emphasis, which allows staff to come into particular hamlets or villages on a planned basis (Cawkwell, 1989).

78

Targetting

There will be times when a fieldworker, agency or team has to be very clear on what basis one or more villages are being targetted. The choice should never be haphazard. As a general rule, an agency should scan local newspapers and keep in touch with its immediate network of supporters and contacts, thereby maintaining a baseline of awareness about issues to which it may decide to respond in particular localities. It can then refer to one or more of the following to help it decide where it will place scarce community work resources:

(i) *Demand*. A community group specifically requests an agency to allocate some of the time of a community worker to it because it wishes to take up a particular issue – obtaining low-cost housing in a commuter village, for example, or improving transport.

(ii) *Social and economic indicators*. Where there is evidence of rural poverty and deprivation the case for providing support to community groups may be strong. Equally, community work inputs may be urgently needed either where depopulation is occurring or where pressures on rural life resulting from, say, urban incomers are acute.

(iii) *The topic or issue*. A rural agency may have experience of a particular topic or of a working method which means that, on the grounds of cost effectiveness, offering a community work input makes sense. If, for example, there is expertise within the agency on setting up computer-based information systems or on launching a community enterprise then this may influence the decision as to what to focus on. We would include here the carrying-out of village appraisals (ACRE, 1989). This has become a well-known way of assessing all aspects of a village. Various materials – such as the 'Local Jigsaw' package in Wales – are available to help do them.

(iv) *Strong leadership*. Committed, experienced local leaders are crucial to focused, indirect work. When they are seen to be present, perhaps through their attendance at a conference, then the argument for a community work input may be strong.

Sometimes the community worker must have confidence that strong leadership will emerge at a later stage and proceed with the intervention on that assumption. This may present him or her with the dilemma of whether to intervene where there are already good local leaders, or in areas which may have needs but where there is a dearth of local leaders. It might be called the 'need versus potential' dilemma.

(v) *Local support*. Through its networks and contacts, a rural agency will often be aware that, within and around several villages or parishes, there is interest and potential support from local staff of other agencies and professionals. This can become a critically important ingredient for the community worker, given that she can only give limited time to working in an area and will need to rely on local professionals – priest, health visitor, doctor – in addition to indigenous leaders. This point is also made in the handbook for organisers and tutors of village-based community development courses produced by ACRE's Rural Adult Education Project (Scott *et al.*, 1989). The authors advise the setting-up of a course planning group at an early stage, and for the inclusion on it of interested parties. The existence or not of such people may determine where, across an area, it makes sense to run a course.

The above five broad indicators must obviously be refined by each community development agency and worker. The indicators require material to be collected from a variety of sources: official statistics on, for example, unemployment and poor-quality housing may be a starting-point. However, they are rarely sufficient, for several reasons:

—— Data at a district, travel-to-work area, or county level are not sufficiently refined to identify individual villages, or clusters of them, which are in greater need.

—— Official statistics do not usually tell you what you need to know. They tend to record the level of known demand for a service (for example, the number of social services clients, or the size of a council house waiting list), rather than the level and nature of the need. They are even less reliable in rural areas, due to the lack of 'penetration' by remote and urban-based public agencies, and to a reluctance of rural people to 'register' their needs.

—— They do not necessarily contribute to understanding. It is important to know not only the measured level of a problem, but also how local people perceive and respond to that problem. Even within a single rural county, there may well be marked differences in the significance of what, for example, a 5 per cent unemployment level actually means: whether it is widely accepted as a problem; whether people are expected to cope with it individually, without fuss; whether the numbers and the people involved make any collective response viable.

The agency and worker therefore need to supplement this information from other sources: their own knowledge and feelings; the take-up by different communities of particular services and opportunities offered by the agency; extrapolation from research findings, newspaper articles and TV reports relating to other, but broadly similar, communities elsewhere in the region or county. The use of quantitative and qualitative indicators to target and focus one's work is not an exact science, but this does not mean that it should be rejected. Agencies and workers need to make choices based on evidence, choices which can be explained and justified to others. To avoid the issue at this stage of the work runs the risk of sapping energy and resources and, in the longer term, of losing credibility and effectiveness.

There may be opportunities for an agency to see its selection of focused work as pilot projects. In other words, there will be an element of evaluating the outcomes and learning gained from a time-limited intervention in order to apply them elsewhere. We have seen that this was the intention behind the choice of areas in Northern Ireland's Rural Action Project.

Two further general points need to be made about focused, indirect work. Firstly, while we think that it is essential that such work be time-limited, in the sense that the worker has a definite withdrawal point, there is no reason why the amount of time given to any one group or project should not sometimes be generous. As we shall see, the worker must have the skills to work sensitively and on a collaborative basis in a community, and the process of applying such skills cannot be short-circuited.

One of the development officers for Yorkshire RCC covered both South and West Yorkshire, and was involved with the villages of Slaithwaite and Marsden in the Upper Colne Valley on a regular basis. Her work there included supporting a community association in Marsden undertaking a major project to convert the Mechanics Institute into a multi-purpose community centre, and involvement with the Upper Colne Valley Trust, an economic-led regeneration initiative. Members of both groups felt that the worker was accessible, even though her work in the valley constituted only one of several local commitments she had in different parts of her area.

Another example is a Children's Society community worker in Mid-Wales. She covered Newtown and the five surrounding rural parishes. She had a brief to explore the church's involvement with communities, so that she was involved with church structures in addition to supporting community groups. The latter included playschemes, a woman's group, a group arguing for new day services for people with learning difficulties and an association of organisations working with children.

Her practice is particularly interesting because she tried to work on a short-term contract basis with specific groups within a wide geographical area, thereby placing her in the focused, indirect strand of our model, at the same time as leaving space to do development work at village level – the direct community work strand. We felt that her job brief put her in the first of these, but that local needs drew her towards the second. It was only by adopting a disciplined but active approach to the first that she was able to open up the second.

The second general point to make about focused, indirect work is that we tend to assume that it relates to a geographical area. This need not always be the case. We think it can be applied at times to groups whose membership reflects a common plight, concern or interest – although admittedly the evidence here is weaker than it is for work in geographical areas. But workers supporting environmental groups, travellers, single-parents groups, alcoholism groups and language groups are equally prone to falling into the trap of not making hard decisions about time allocation as they are when working with village-based groups. The principles behind the idea of focused, indirect work apply just as powerfully.

Process

Of the three elements of the rural community work model, focused, indirect work needs to be the most tightly defined in terms of time commitment and boundaries for any work undertaken. The following stages of the process seek to reflect these deliberate constraints:

(i) *Selection of community*. As we have seen, choice of area or issue on which to work presents considerable difficulties. This is both because of the problem of deciding the criteria or indicators to use in reaching such a decision, and also because it means that the worker and agency are forced into prioritising some commitments above others.

(ii) *Getting accepted*. This too is a very testing area for the worker, especially if she is not from the area herself. The danger is that, in the concern to keep to schedule, this part of the process will be rushed. This can have negative results: disillusion among local leaders, even their alienation from the worker or agency concerned.

(iii) *Setting the contract.* Among some community workers, agreeing a contract – usually verbal rather than written – between a worker and a group is not seen to be appropriate. A free-flowing, flexible approach is preferred, one which relies on mutual respect, trust and affinity, more than anything approaching the idea of a contract. Indeed, some would argue that introducing a contract at the delicate early stages of a group's life is poor practice: it cuts across notions of goodwill and commitment which the worker is seeking to encourage.

We have every sympathy for this perspective but, in situations where an approach akin to focused, indirect work is being advanced, we think that the free-flowing perspective has to give way to a more contractual relationship. Accordingly, setting the contract becomes a vitally important piece of business done between a worker and local leaders. It has to establish what kind of support the worker will offer, over what period of time, and with what probable outcomes. The contract will need to convey the level of flexibility which will be possible, as well as the time-scale for this level of work.

(iv) *Providing support.* Over an agreed period of time, the worker has regular contact with individuals. She will tend to work through them, in place of the whole group which lies beyond them, with which she will have only occasional direct contact. She will be deliberately trying to encourage action, whether that be the forma- tion of a group, the clarifying of an issue or support of a few individuals. It is at the heart of the process in the sense that it is when substantive community work is done.

(v) *Withdrawal.* The worker brings her involvement with local leaders to an end. They – and the groups they may be representing – have received their support from the community worker, whose time is released to do work elsewhere.

(vi) *Keeping in touch.* It is essential that leaders can contact the worker when necessary. This may be in order to clarify the earlier advice given by the worker or to report on progress. It may take the form of correspondence or a telephone call. The worker will be alert to any tendency to being drawn back in to a major involvement.

The following sketches of workers or agencies undertaking focused, indirect work emphasise different aspects of the above process:

Limavady Community Development Initiative

This is a voluntary organisation based in the small town of Limavady in the north-west of Northern Ireland. It was set up as an initiative of the district youth office, and was funded by the Training Agency to provide training and work experience for unemployed people. The organiser was an experienced community worker who was anxious to develop an enabling role for the project alongside its predominantly servicing functions: welfare rights work, community care work and community service. Its premises were in the town centre, and the organiser had been aware of the relatively few applications she received from the surrounding settlements for jobs at the centre. The one consistent request received from the rural areas was for advice on village halls.

The project received a request from the tenants' association of a small village (thirty-eight houses) for a worker to help it with administration. The organiser made several visits to the village to meet those involved and find out more about the request. Eventually she explained that the tenants' association on its own could not justify having a worker, but that if it got together with other groups the resource could be made available. A meeting, to which twenty people came, was held and the Limavady organiser explained how a community advice centre could work and what administration was involved.

The initiative 'took off' from there. The council gave a grant of £1000 and the centre received the support of one-and-a-half workers. The involvement of the organiser, which had been intensive, finished, except for the support and supervision she gave to the workers. An important additional element to her work, which reflected the policy of the Limavady project, was the achievement of having both Protestants and Catholics as members of the advice centre committee.

Association of Community Enterprises in the Highlands and Islands (ACE-HI)

Since the end of the 1970s the Highlands and Islands Development Board had supported the creation and development of community co-operatives. With the disappearance in 1983 of funds to retain the HIDB fieldworkers there was a vacuum: no back-up or source of information to support community enterprises. That was why they came together in 1985 to form ACE-HI.

Most of ACE-HI's work fits the first strand of our model – working from a distance. The organisation covers a very large area, much of it consisting of sparsely populated islands, and it has been essential for the organisation to develop effective ways of working from a distance. However, it is also aware that the real difficulties associated with establishing viable co-operatives in communities, which are both economically and socially fragile, requires an additional dimension. It has sought to achieve this by supporting the community development elements underpinning successful co-operatives. It has helped run training courses in a small number of areas, and provided direct support to co-operatives at critical stages in their development.

Thus we can see that ACE-HI has resisted being cast purely in the co-ordinating, information and representative/lobby mode. It is concerned to use some of its staff resources to become involved with key individuals in co-operatives and other enterprise initiatives for limited periods of time. For example, an ACE-HI development worker assisted the Community Enterprise Group of Milton, a village near Invergordon, to compile a detailed community profile, and the volunteers from the group received training through ACE-HI (Corner, 1989). In this way, it demonstrated specific support to its members, realising, in the words of its first chairman, that 'the effects of a failure can be far more drastic in a rural area than in an urban area' (Justad, 1986).

Berwickshire Girls Work Project

This was a specially funded, two-year project to look at provision for girls in the district's youth clubs and elsewhere. It was initiated by two agencies – the Berwickshire Association of Youth Clubs and the Eastern Borders Community Education Team.

The project workers undertook a survey of girls in youth clubs and secondary schools, ran a girls' day, did group work with girls in clubs and organised a residential for girls. Thus there was a need for extensive contact-making and networking. The initiative enabled the team to obtain useful information, especially concerning the difficulties faced by girls in villages of attending clubs – one of the project report's conclusions was that 'particularly in rural areas young women need positive discrimination in their favour so they can reach their fullest potential' (Berwickshire Girls Work Project, 1988).

The project was a good example of how professional workers from different agencies can collaborate in a well-planned and imaginative way. They were aware of the problems and restrictions facing girls in rural areas and, within a set time-period, they worked with youth leaders and others on a specified programme. It illustrates how the concept of focused, indirect work can be applied to an interest group as well as to geographical areas. Both elements are present in *Doing by Learning* (Scott *et al.*, 1989), the handbook for organisers and tutors of village-based community development courses which exemplifies the focused, indirect approach. The article by Sarah Banks (1990) on adult education and rural community development raises similar questions. Her assessment of two projects in rural County Durham suggests that a targetted approach, in this case via adult education, can achieve participation; it can mean that courses are brought to areas where none, or very few, have been available.

Activities

(i) *Targetting particular communities.* This is about making choices between different communities. The focus may be a particular geographical area, a type of community, or an issue.

(ii) *Creating opportunities to work with particular communities or groups.* Targetting implies a conscious choice by the agency or worker to focus on a particular community, based on available information. However, focusing can also be achieved by creating appropriate opportunities for communities to select themselves. This does not have to be a totally random and haphazard process. The opportunities can be created in a variety of ways: through organising a competition for the most innovative community-based initiative in the district; by running a grant-aid scheme to help new initiatives get off the ground; by developing and publicising the offer of a specialist advice service linked to a particular priority issue or activity.

(iii) *Working with and beyond key actors.* In the chapter on rural communities we discussed the role of key actors in communities who are, on the one hand, a resource because of their connections, skills, accepted wisdom, and, on the other, a possible barrier to effective involvement by the worker with the community beyond them. Focused indirect work requires the careful identification and selection of key actors, both actual and potential. Possibly obstructive gatekeepers may also need to be involved in the community work process: they cannot always be circumvented or ignored.

However, these actors do not have to be taken at face value. The approach involves cultivating, motivating, educating and supporting them, in the processes, skills, knowledge, values and culture of community work. It is the actors themselves, rather than the worker, who then work with groups and individuals in the community. These processes are crucial to focused, indirect work, and they call on the community worker to wield and impart a range of skills and techniques such as providing structured training and personal support, negotiation, diplomacy and management.

(iv) *Broadening people's agendas.* Most groups are constituted for specific purposes, and few become involved spontaneously in community development, although they all to varying degrees possess the potential to do so. The existence of these groups can be a resource rather than a barrier to wider community involvement. Focused, indirect work can challenge and motivate groups to think and act more widely, resourcefully and imaginatively.

In some cases these groups will welcome this stimulation. In other cases, a group may be less prepared or forthcoming, and community workers need to exercise care not to alienate themselves from the group by being too demanding, pushy or unrealistic. The challenge to community workers is in making the judgement as to whether a particular group can fulfil a particular role and, if so, how much investment of worker time and resources may be needed to help the group achieve it.

(v) *Effective withdrawal.* Because focused, indirect work with a particular community involves an end, as well as a beginning, of fairly intensive involvement by the worker, the final stages need to be planned and negotiated in advance. In that way the group can be left in a reasonably self-supporting state, not in a high state of dependency with expectations suddenly left unfulfilled. This requires not only the development of individuals and mechanisms within the community to carry on after the worker has ceased active involvement, but also the establishment of an effective working-from-a-distance support mechanism by the agency to make longer-term support available when needed.

Focused, indirect work requires the practitioner to have some face-to-face contact with local people beyond a one-off meeting. This is the main point of differentiation between it and working from a distance. Yet the contact will be rationed, and the worker will have to use methods and techniques which convey this message from the start.

Inevitably, it will be a mixed message: on the one hand the worker wishes to be of service to rural communities, on the other he or she is stating that only a limited resource is available. Accordingly, ways need to be found of making the worker accessible while at the same time ensuring that his or her time and energy is protected. One practice is for the worker to let it be known on which day or days of the week she will be in the village. That can be part of the contract, and it will be reinforced by the worker's adherence to it.

Knowing how to negotiate a contract with local leaders is essential for the community worker. It is about reaching an agreement as to (a) how long the worker will be involved – this could be on the basis of a set time-period or until certain tasks have been achieved – and (b) the nature of the worker's involvement: what she will be doing, any resources she will bring, how often she will visit, where she can be contacted. An equally important skill for effective focused, indirect work is that of setting priorities, and it may be necessary for an agency to provide training opportunities for staff in this and related management techniques and skills.

Another method is for the community worker to be linked to a mobile resource, such as an information and advice service or library, which visits clusters of villages on a regular basis. There is substantial experience of mobile information and advice services, and the literature usefully opens up the community work dimension. For example, in their case study of a mobile information and action van in West Cumbria, Butcher *et al.* (1976) link their findings to the issue of the extent of informal helping networks in village communities. And the report on Northumberland's Rural Information Service (Lumb, 1989) states that:

> The principles of the service were to take a wide range of information to people in rural areas and to raise awareness of the sources which are available...Without easy access to information rural people tend not to be aware of their rights as citizens or of who can help them if they are in difficulties.

From this we can see that, in addition to offering a framework on which to base his or her presence in a community, a mobile service also holds the potential of opening up new spheres of work for the community worker. One of the follow-up initiatives in the Northumberland project was a community development approach in one village because statistics and the bus workers' reports showed evidence of a high level of both personal and community problems there.

ACRE's briefing kit (1988), on identifying people's information and advice needs, makes the point that link-persons and volunteer contacts in villages need to be properly selected and trained in information and advice giving. In sparsely inhabited areas, such people are often likely to be those on whom the community worker will rely for practising focused, indirect work. That is, the same people will be both a local point of contact for dispersing information, and a starting point for stimulating community activities.

If one of the keys to this practice lies in the management of a worker's accessibility, the other is in using methods which seek to help make links between leaders and active members of groups across a wide geographical area. This takes further the information sharing and linking work identified for working from a distance: focused, indirect work will actively seek to help members of different groups both to learn from each other and to work together on joint projects and campaigns. Efforts made by a worker to make these connections can be seen as providing an alternative support system: as a group's semi-dependence on the worker is broken, so a new source of help is suggested. Such provision can be vital if a group is planning to embark on a transport or housing campaign, where a case has to be made with painstaking care over a long period of time. Doing this alongside groups in other areas, co-ordinating plans and sharing resources can make the difference between success or failure.

Skills

In addition to using face-to-face skills, the community worker will need to have available most of the same resources required as when working from a distance: telephone, newsletter, use of local press and radio, libraries and exhibitions, computers. In order to make themselves known to far-flung and isolated villages and settlements, community workers may need to consider gaining newspaper publicity as well as using public notice boards (e.g. in sub-post offices) and leaflets and posters. It is important to guard against the tendency for community work resources to be used, and effectively monopolised, by those leaders who know about them.

Focused, indirect work can usually be practised effectively by a generalist worker: someone who has community work experience and skills and who feels comfortable working on his or her own.

Occasionally, however, the nature of the 'contract' between a worker and a community may require the input of expertise in a particular area – housing, transport, employment, etc. In that instance, because the approach does not assume a long time-scale, it may be important for the community worker to practise jointly with a specialist. The latter person would bring special skills or knowledge which would feed directly into the plans of a group or organisation.

A worker's ability to practise shared working may require encouragement. The pairing may be as equal partners, in which the amount of time given is shared. But that assumes that there are generous staff resources available. Thus, the more likely situation is of the community worker and her agency arranging with another agency for an expert to provide advice – again on a time-limited basis. The skill of paired work lies in identifying clearly the ways in which the two workers will complement each other, in knowing when such an approach is needed, and in specifying the point it will come into play and for how long.

Underlying the skills required for focused, indirect work is the ability to mobilise and acquire resources. These may be from other workers or agencies, and they will certainly include the resource – and resourcefulness – of local leaders. Since the practitioner's intervention is targetted and time-limited, the need for him or her to be seen to deliver is crucial. The skills, it might be said, have to be applied in a businesslike way.

At the same time, the skills have to be used with considerable awareness of the customs and expectations of local communities. The worker will need to be adept at striking up collaborative ways of working with local leaders, at the same time as making it clear that the community work intervention will be time-limited. It would be disastrous for the worker, in his or her enthusiasm to maintain an effective form of practice, to cut across acceptable ways of doing things in small, face-to-face communities. In his analysis of nine projects in rural England, Benfield (1990) accepts the necessity for 'working with the grain':

> Initial contacts were made via and through the existing leadership. Although this pre-determined, and thus narrowed, the range of contacts available to the worker and issues she could take up, it was the only quick way of gaining entry and establishing legitimacy in small rural communities where the leadership could effectively obstruct the progress of the worker.

In criticising the projects for having failed to engage with issues of deprivation, Benfield highlights a major challenge for the focused, indirect approach.

Role

The role of the worker in focused, indirect work comes close to classic descriptions of the enabling capacity of the community worker:

> He is a person who helps people look at themselves, to look below the surface and probe their deepest feelings about community, i.e. he encourages verbalisation of these feelings, he helps people see the commonality of their feelings, he nourishes the hope that something can be done collectively about these. (Ross and Lappin, 1967)

The worker's role is constrained by the need to be focused and work through a limited number of individuals. This, in our opinion, predisposes her to adopt an explicitly directive role. Having won the trust of leaders in a community, and having gained entry, she will need to relate to people in ways which convey clear messages as to what she intends to achieve. She will be letting contacts know the knowledge and expertise she can provide or obtain and she will take an active role in ensuring that agreed objectives are reached.

An insight into the role was given to us by the worker on the Derwentside Patchwork Project in County Durham. She was based in an office of the planning department, outside the patch, and became involved with several villages and projects. She was clear that her job did not involve 'handholding' community groups: 'If there is a problem, they get in touch.' Furthermore it was essential for her to work closely with the formal system – clerks of parish councils, secretaries of community associations and Women's Institutes branches. She described herself as 'an enabler of people who want to do things', and was anxious not to be drawn into side issues. She was aware that people often have a low level of awareness of what agencies can provide. Most of the time she felt she was working on behalf of local people rather than with them. She could only do this if she had their trust.

Within the directiveness of the worker's role there is often a strong advisory element. He or she is someone from outside a local community who is being looked to for information and guidance. In this sense the worker is seen by local leaders as an expert. The role is frequently manifest in the support given to village community care groups – volunteers who offer a range of services. Commenting on the work of care group advisors in Hampshire, Armstrong and Thompson (1986) note that they are

> drawing in informal village networks, helping to co-ordinate them more effectively and providing backup and support. The care group advisors also act as a link between the groups and the statutory services and help ensure that groups are not asked to substitute for statutory services.

The worker's role must help local people to 'move things on', so that all concerned are aware that the worker is bringing tangible benefits to a plan or project. If it is accepted that this approach requires the worker to play a directive role, the reader can legitimately ask: how is this done? What are the attributes of directiveness? The degrees of directiveness given by Rothman (1969) are:

Channelling (strongly directive):
   'The practitioner asserts a particular point of view with supporting argument and documentation. He channels thinking directly towards a given goal.'

Funnelling (considerably directive):
   'This practitioner gives a range of possible choices and subtly funnels thinking in a given direction by asserting his preference for a particular goal and the rationale for that choice.'

Scanning (mildly directive):
   'This practitioner scans the range of possibilities related to solving a particular problem, presenting them impartially and on the basis of parity. He provides an orientation to goal selection, setting out the boundaries within which possible rational goal selection may take place.'

We see, therefore, that directiveness requires the community worker to 'lead from the front'; he or she is less the listener, more the exponent of a choice of views on tactics, action and resources. This is unfamiliar territory for most British community workers, and will often require a deliberate change of attitude and behaviour. Accordingly, appropriate opportunities for training and support, and for the worker to evaluate the directive role with other workers or a consultant, will be essential.

It is a role which will greatly test the confidence of the worker because, on the face of things, it sits uneasily alongside traditional community work values. Yet when used effectively the benefits it can deliver, in a relatively short period of time, are tangible and considerable. Furthermore, it is important not to equate directiveness with authoritarianism or rigidity. We are arguing that this role is appropriate for the worker who is practising focused, indirect work, but she must do this within a framework of values which are consonant with community work.

Concluding remarks

In the village of Waunfawr there has been a scheme for integrating people with learning difficulties into the community. The project's chairman was a member of the Secretary of State for Wales working party on the All Wales Strategy for Mental Handicap. As a result of struggling not to have his handicapped son 'put away' he became – in his own words – an agitator. He and other villagers organised themselves, and mobilised considerable external resources (see Johnstone *et al.*, 1990, p. 113; and *Antur Waunfawr*, undated). This was an example where community work skills from outside the locality were not needed, and of course there are hundreds of other situations where similar amounts of energy and commitment have produced effective self-help schemes.

Yet there are also occasions where a time-limited community work intervention is crucial. Focused, indirect work provides a framework for this, a set of working principles on which an agency or worker strategy can be based and which indicates the knowledge, skills and techniques required.

The essence of the approach is partnership, an agreement between a worker and a community or community group on the human and other resources which each can offer. It is an approach which cannot be wholly demand-led, in the sense of a worker or agency simply responding to requests for help. Yet nor is it a worker- or agency-dominated intervention. This is a point brought out strongly by Lumb (1990) in her case study of a village appraisal in the North Pennine settlement of Allenheads:

The real skill in development work is in seeing which approach will best help the community concerned, and the demands and expectations of other organisations are part of the context in which the tools of rural development work are selected and used.

Finally, we emphasise again that this and the two other strands of the model are not mutually exclusive. If we return to the example given at the beginning of this chapter, we are reminded of the need for agencies to plan to use, move between and integrate all three strands:

> where we target our help elsewhere will depend to some extent on our existing commitments.... In view of the fact that many of the village appraisals are being triggered by an upsurge in population pressure (usually by the submission of a large residential planning application) we could expect increased interest from all but the most remote rural communities in the county. However, in view of our firm commitment to the remoter rural areas, we must be careful not to become too wrapped up in responding to demands from the pressured areas. (Community Council of Northumberland, 1990)

7

Direct Community Work

The opportunities for the community worker who undertakes direct work to become involved in a community are enormous. Having the time to meet people, for the worker to get to know them and vice versa, gives an undoubted distinctiveness to this strand of the model. On the other hand, direct community work is not a licence for a worker to blend wholly into the lives and culture of rural people. Nor should it be assumed that direct work necessarily requires a worker to be based in a community for an unbounded period of time; quite the contrary, precisely because direct work contains within it the danger of being too open-ended, there is a need for it to be formulated, practised and evaluated with rigour. That may include time-limited commitment by the worker.

Fundamental to good practice of direct community work is empathy with the values and culture of rural communities. For this to be possible, the worker will need to have a high degree of awareness of, and respect for, how local people think, talk and behave. Only in this way will she gain the trust she needs in order to be able to practise direct community work effectively. In earlier chapters we pointed to key elements lying within rural communities – conservatism, suspicion of outsiders, the hold of individualism, a degree of fatalism – and it is with these in mind that we stress the need for the worker to be sensitive to patterns of behaviour and to identify with local culture:

> It is important to learn how to use local social networks. It was the experience of the projects in Northern Ireland and Ikaria that it takes two years to establish a working knowledge of local networks and culture. It may be important to attend local church services, help in the fields, sing in the cafes and pubs etc. (Kennedy and Kelleher, 1989)

95

The overlay of public and private lives is present in many communities, but it can be especially evident in traditional villages. In attempting direct community work, the worker has, to some extent, to become part of this inter-twining. She has to get inside the networks, social relationships, informal gatherings – not to lose her community worker identity or deny her role, but so as to gain acceptance and eventual credibility. The term 'invisible trust networks' is used sometimes to describe this process. It will unfold in different ways and, because it deals with a web of new, intangible elements, there are no clear pathways for the worker to follow. Only general guidance can be given. What is certain is that the 'closeness' of rural communities is an aspect of community work with which a worker must engage. Martinez-Brawley (1982) makes a similar observation about working in many American rural communities:

> Nowhere is the social work practitioner more inter-related to the community than in the rural areas.... Furthermore, the personal and professional life of the social workers cannot be detached from community commitments, particularly if one resides in the rural area served.

Process

> Family feuds, village rivalries, the existence of clearly recognised social hierarchies and the personal fear of failure in communities renowned for long memories, are all factors that bring their own complexities to bear on a process that is neither clearly understood nor openly articulated. (Rural Action Project, 1989)

The process of direct community work needs to be differentiated from the urban-based neighbourhood work process described by Alan Twelvetrees (1991), Paul Henderson and David Thomas (1987) and others. We have suggested already that the two main reasons for this have to do with the nature of rurality and rural communities, and with timescale. Kennedy and Kelleher (1989) may exaggerate a little when they state that the timescale involved in initiating, implementing and consolidating a rural project takes approximately seven years, and 'it can take up to twenty years to develop a climate of participation which is accepted by the local community and other levels of local and national government', but the spirit behind what they say is right.

The following process model seeks to take account of the rural and timescale factors. Some of the stages are identified by the same terms as those in urban neighbourhood work, yet the meaning may differ in important ways. Other stages in the following nine-stage process are unique to rural work. It is not a sequential process and it is worker, not group, focused. There is no suggestion that a worker ceases involvement with one stage of the process as he or she moves on to the next. It is put forward as a framework or guide for workers and managers to plan, carry out and evaluate direct community work. From a glance, it can be seen that the early stages of the process have a strong emphasis on the worker meeting people and gaining acceptance:

(i) *Deciding where to practice.* This decision, which is often made before the community worker is appointed, is of crucial importance. Not only must a rational choice, based on an assessment of need or the salience of an issue, be made; but also care has to be taken as to how the decision is made public. A nightmare for a management committee is a headline in the local newspaper announcing that a special worker is to be assigned to a named village. Community work has always to struggle against reinforcing the negative labelling of communities, no more so than in those rural communities which have a tradition of pride and self-reliance. Where possible, choosing a locality in collaboration with one or more local leaders is strongly advisable. It will help prepare the community for the worker's arrival. How the decision-making is handled is likely to influence significantly the future opportunities of the community worker, one way or another.

(ii) *Entering the community.* This is the stage where local people get the opportunity to meet the worker. Being introduced by 'gatekeepers' is usually sensible and helpful: one or more local people who, because they know other local people and the community worker, can effect appropriate meetings. It is a part of the job where the community worker is both listening to the opinions and experiences of the people he meets, and explaining who he is and what his job is. It is important for the worker to resist any temptation to begin working up action plans; people need time to absorb the ingredients of the job, and the worker must plan his interventions rather than rely upon instinct.

It is important to emphasise again the point concerning the curiosity of rural people about an incomer who intends to work in their community. Thus the worker has to be ready to say a bit about herself – her interests, where she lives, her family and her previous jobs etc. One community worker told us that, when starting work in a farming area of Staffordshire, she gained extra credibility because she herself had been brought up in a Yorkshire farming community. As soon as the community worker arrives, she is highly visible and needs to be able to explain her presence immediately.

(iii) *Getting to know the community.* This is a familiar part of community work practice-theory. It has to do with collecting data from a variety of sources. Yet whereas the urban community worker can often retain his or her anonymity while finding out about a neighbourhood, this is much less likely in the rural context. It is essential for the worker to be sensitive to this reality (see Chapter 2). It may mean that some of the methods used in urban settings, such as street interviews and reading council minutes, will need to be limited. Otherwise, the worker will risk needlessly arousing local anxieties and suspicion.

(iv) *Gaining trust.* The stage of gaining trust locally is closely linked with the two previous stages. Gaining trust is a constant theme throughout the process, but it is quite fundamental at the point that a worker begins to create the foundations of her work. We insert it as a distinct stage in the process, not through false optimism that it can be secured as a result of applying skills and techniques and having the right personality, but because it needs to be at the forefront of the community worker's mind at this point.

One way of building trust is for the worker to carry out tasks in a community. They may be quite small – obtaining a new list of equipment for the playgroup organiser, driving an elderly person to hospital – but they will convey important messages to local people: this person is interested in our community, she comes here regularly, she is easy to talk with and she can be relied upon to do things for us.

(v) *Making contacts.* This is the stage where the community worker moves into a more strategic mode. She should be asking herself, why do I want to meet this or that person, and how do they and their concerns fit into a way forward? Again, we underline the need for the worker to ensure that she keeps listening to what people say to her, clues they may give about possible issues, a new slant on the history and experiences of villagers. And when she offers information about resources she must be certain to deliver:

Any information the Patchworker is asked for should be available to the contact as soon as possible, to help reinforce their picture of the Patchworker as an 'information provider' and as a professional. (Standing Conference of Rural Community Councils, 1986)

Many community workers also emphasise the need to seek a broad range of contacts from the beginning; otherwise there is the danger that they will be seen to be aligned with only one network or social class:

It is advisable that she/he is and seen to be, autonomous from the more 'elitist' networks of the areas and to avoid being associated with any particular 'clique'. (Kennedy and Kelleher, 1989)

If over-identification occurs in the early stages of direct community work, it is easy for the worker to be 'locked in' to one group of people, and he or she can find it very hard to move to a wider constituency.

(vi) *Working with individuals.* We are convinced that effective direct community work depends on the worker establishing close ties with small numbers of individuals. The relationship may be predominantly functional, in that it is directed towards realising or supporting group action, but it may also be more personal in that the worker encourages the development of individuals – helping them become more skilled, challenging assumptions, widening horizons.

(vii) *Working with groups and organisations.* 'The important role for the community worker is in providing a link between the community and the powers that be' (Justad, 1990). The community worker operates both inside a community and outside of it, with those organisations whose policies impinge on it. He or she may need to facilitate the development of new groups, be involved with the on-going organisations – parish council, playgroup, village hall committee – and also work with local authorities, economic development agencies, health authorities, and county-wide voluntary organisations.

It is crucial for the worker to get the right emphasis, in terms of workload, between these three – new community groups, existing groups and professional agencies. If he or she is drawn in to too much liaison work with external agencies there is the danger that he/she will lose the close relationship with local people which is the essence of this strand of rural community work. The liaison is undertaken in order to support communities, not as something in its own right.

(viii) *Building support systems.* A worker must anticipate his or her withdrawal from a community. The stage of building-in support to on-going work should be experienced as having evolved out of planned practice, not as an unexpected demand. It may well take the form of encouraging and training one or more local people to take on aspects of the worker's role once he or she has gone. Or it may require work at a structural level, especially the creation of mechanisms for contact between a community and the local authority.

(ix) *Leavings and endings.* Direct community work seeks to work closely with individuals and groups, and it is probably inevitable that there will be an element of dependency – on both sides. Thus it is particularly important to pay attention to good practice about preparing to leave, and about ending a presence and friendship which has been intensive.

Activities

(i) *Building trust, confidence and relationships with and between all parts of the community.* The concept of community work will almost certainly be unknown to the community, and so the credibility and legitimacy of the worker must be based on their own personality and background rather than any ascribed status arising from professional qualifications or agency base. Getting to know and understand the community is essential: what makes it tick; which are the groups, factors, networks; where, and on what basis, are the affinities and conflicts; who are the people with power and influence, and how do they operate; what are the values which underpin people's place in the community; what are the issues, and what has been the history of activity within the community. This process of getting to know and understand the community goes hand-in-hand with the building of trust, confidence and relationships with the community.

(ii) *Strengthening and building groups.* The intensity and intimacy of direct work allows the worker to assess the strengths and weaknesses of existing groups, and to facilitate the creation of new groups and relationships. Existing groups may be well placed to further the community work objectives, but may need nurturing and support to become active. Alternatively, they may be non-existent in a community, or completely inappropriate to the task, and so the worker may need to concentrate on building new groups. This brings challenges both for securing the involvement of people who may not normally participate in group activities, and in working around existing groups and actors.

(iii) *Facilitating the creation of a strategy.* Communities, and groups within them, do not readily think and organise themselves strategically. Indeed, a rural community which values tradition and continuity may feel quite uncomfortable with the concepts of organisation and strategy.

However, if community groups and people within them are to move forward, they do need to clarify the issues: just what it is they are trying to achieve; decide which matters are a priority; how they are going to make progress. This process may involve a structured specification of goals, objectives and priorities, or it may be done in a less formal, but still purposeful way. It depends on such factors as what the people themselves feel comfortable with, how much formality or structure is needed to achieve the necessary clarity, whether it is needed to satisfy some external requirements (e.g. the potential funder of a community project). The skill of the community worker is to help people not only to develop a sense of strategy, but also to do this in a way which is appropriate to the community.

(iv) *Putting ideas into action.* To implement a strategy or take action to meet identified needs may seem the natural and spontaneous core of the community work process, but it may need the community worker's involvement both to happen at all and to work well. A considerable challenge to the worker is to facilitate this process, rather than to do it herself. Pointing people in the direction of resources (money, technical expertise, appropriate agencies, etc.) is a key activity, as is helping people to overcome setbacks, to deal with conflicts, and generally to learn through doing.

A further challenge for the worker may be to help communities to see when ideas should *not* be put into action: for example, deciding not to proceed with an over-ambitious village hall building project. Similarly, a worker has to be adept at helping people to end projects – either when they are achieved or when they are shown not to be viable.

(v) *Refreshment and regeneration.* Community-based action is not a simple process of beginning, middle and ending, but rather a complex overlay of relationships, processes, highs and lows, false starts, dashed hopes, successes, bursts of enthusiasm, vision. The community worker is involved in this complexity: spurring people on when spirits are low, encouraging fresh thinking, creating challenge, promoting participation and compassion, caring and sharing, helping to see things not only as they are, but how they could be. The aim is to do this in a way which does not make individuals totally dependent on the worker, but rather helps them eventually to stand on their own – interdependent – feet.

There needs to be a risk factor in the practice of direct community work. What we mean by this is a working principle which keeps to the forefront the objective of seeing that key issues are addressed: poverty, housing, unemployment, mental illness. In many instances, a community worker may feel caught in a dilemma between the need to respect the customs and uniqueness of a community, and the drive to expose difficult 'hidden' issues and see that they are worked on.

Engaging with 'hidden' issues

This is a tension which was experienced by the Rural Action Project in Northern Ireland. Its brief was to focus on groupings or communities which had been identified as being poor. Yet communities often rejected the stigma of poverty. RAP's evaluator raised the issue in the following terms:

> The two crucial issues as far as the European Programme is concerned are – how to deal with such a wide and dispersed territory with a small team of staff; and how to maintain the focus on poverty within the rural areas when some of the issues raised through the community development process will undoubtedly reflect the interests of the better-off farmers or developers. (Benington, 1989)

Yet the 'tough' issues have to be addressed. Otherwise community work will amount to very little. Deciding when and how to do this is the point at which the community worker has to take risks – that local people and community leaders with whom she is working will be surprised, shaken, made angry because she appears to be disturbing the status quo. The risk is of losing the wider constituency for the work. In many English villages it will be members of the parish council, village society, parochial church council, Women's Institute: established organisations which can, if they wish, make life very difficult for a community worker.

What we are raising appears to cast doubt on the consensus politics with which rural community work is strongly aligned. However, it is important not to equate the principle of reaching out to 'non-joiners' and the disadvantaged with conflict tactics. The challenge of direct community work is to find ways for the practitioner to apply understanding and skills which keep him or her within a broad consensus framework but which also challenge prevailing attitudes and structures.

Working with individuals

Exploring ways of handling the integration draws in again the question of social class, and with which aspects of it the community worker engages. It also helps to clarify another key characteristic of rural community work: the need to work with individuals at the same time as tapping the potential for collective action. We want here to question possibly a central community work tenet, namely that the main purpose and goal is to bring people together and organise them into some form of collective action. Let us consider the following factors:

(a) the prevalence of existing voluntary and community organisa-tions in any one locality;
(b) the small numbers of people, and therefore of potential participants;
(c) problems of distance and communication;
(d) the argument that encouraging people to set up formal associations may run counter to 'communal' tradition, i.e. arising naturally out of people living and working together for many years – 'It is worth speculating on whether, from the locals' point of view, the proliferation of village organisations reflects not so much a flourishing of community life as a symbol of its downfall. (Newby, 1987)

Working with individuals is fundamental to all community work practice. Usually it takes the form of (a) the worker supporting and advising members of community groups who hold key positions – treasurer, chairman – about how to handle and plan their responsi-bilities, and (b) adult education: encouraging the personal develop-ment of individual members of groups, either at a very informal level or by helping them to follow an educational course.

It is the educational component which we believe should be given greater significance than hitherto in direct community work. By this we mean that educational and personal development objectives need to figure explicitly in workers' planning and evaluation, and they themselves need to feel confident and knowledgeable about adult education theories and methodologies. There are implications here for the training and recruitment of community workers.

There is another way in which working with individuals lies at the centre of direct community work. It is a more functional approach than the educational one and can be described best as helping individuals who are outside existing voluntary and community organisations to prepare to play certain parts in those groups. It can take the form of the community worker rehearsing with them situations they will encounter, thereby boosting their self-confidence, enabling them to take risks which are always present when someone is poised to join an existing group. The community worker is almost in the role of a personal tutor, offering support to individuals at different stages.

We are suggesting that work with individuals constitutes a significant component of direct community work. Obviously the worker will initiate and support collective action. Our argument is that this can be brought about in a number of ways and that, in the rural context, work with individuals is mainstream. One should not assume that forming people into a community group is always the paramount concern; community work at a local level can also be practised by working with individuals, only ultimately with a collective end. This, we think, differs from 'mainstream' community work practice-theory. For a related discussion of the differences we recommend the report of the rural research group of the Self-Help Alliance (1988).

Personal involvement

As one worker on my own, the project came to be synonymous with me. My approach was the project's approach. People were more aware that I was around and willing to help with things than that a formal 'project' as such existed. (Hereford and Worcester RCC, 1981)

This was Jackie Denman's experience on the Wyeside project and it reminds us again of the extent to which the worker has to be involved as an individual when practising direct community work.

It is the combination of skills and personality which is all-important, and it is a combination which must be based on strong commitment both to the practice itself and to local people. He or she will be concerned to allay suspicions local people may have of an outsider. The worker will be obliged to show and use his or her personality, in order to get inside the community and gain its trust. On a practical level, this means the worker being accessible and approachable. The indigenous worker is at a big advantage here, and the worker coming from the outside will need to plan this aspect with care. Included in the planning should be the objective of becoming known to a wide range of people: working across the spectrum of social class rather than within only one part of it. In order to survive as a community worker in rural communities, such tactics and politics can be crucial.

Skills

It is all too easy for a worker to be 'frozen out' as a result of pressure from one quarter or another. We are urging workers to recognise this political reality, and present themselves in the community accordingly. Jackie Denman talks about working with two different dimensions at the same time, and it is a theme echoed by several other experienced rural community workers. This, essentially, is about working with both recognised community leaders and with 'ordinary' members of the community. Closely linked to this approach is the need for community workers to be alert to the tendency for many rural people not to separate out the 'professional' from the 'person' – who you are, how you behave. It is within this context that we identify the following skills required for direct community work. Again, we remind the reader that these are not unique to direct work.

(i) *Listening* – this one word contains so much for the rural worker: listening in the sense of watching and interpreting a community – the way it goes about its business; listening in the sense of understanding the concerns or anxieties of particular individuals – giving them time to get to know the worker and share ideas; listening in the sense of receiving lots of different information, storing and recording it, and then using it at later stages: 'The smallest details could often be of great importance later if they could be recalled at the right moment' (Hereford and Worcester RCC, 1981). We note again the emphasis on one-to-one work. There will be existing, mainly established organisations, and it is important for the worker to be listening to these, but much of the day-to-day graft will be visiting individuals and listening to them – with a concern to knit together actual or potential public issues within a community. The skill of listening is fundamental. Implied by it is considerable patience, an enjoyment in meeting people and respecting their points of view, and the time and legitimacy from his or her employing body to apply the skill.

(ii) *Educative* – this can be understood as the logical outcome of effective listening. Having made a relationship, established a basis for dialogue, the worker will be concerned to draw out from people their experience and resources. From there she will want at times to stretch people's horizons. This may be especially important in two extremes of rural community: that which feels itself to be cut off from mainstream society, perhaps with a tradition of deference and conservatism, and that where tensions between locals and incomers are very evident. In the former, the worker will need to use educational skills which stimulate, and give confidence to, local people. In the latter, he or she may need to 'unpack' what may be a crude or over-simple understanding of why the incomers are there, what they contribute to the community, the issues which impact on both locals and incomers.

The informal adult education skills needed for this work complement those identified in *Doing by Learning* (Scott *et al.*, 1989). They also provide a means whereby the community worker can raise questions concerning the 'tough' or 'hidden' issues in rural communities. For example, he or she could discuss the history of a community's experience of poverty, and relate it to today: who in the area may be forced to rely on state benefits, and why? What might be done about it?

(iii) *Facilitating and enabling* – the skills associated with bringing people together and helping them form a community group; or the skills of working with an existing group and helping it to develop. No one could dispute that this kind of support is fundamental to community work. The crucial question is how, in the rural setting, a worker carries it out effectively. From our observations and evidence it is apparent that the key ingredient is the worker's capacity to be sensitive to the subtleties of every situation. Not only are there major differences between types of rural area, but also every community is unique. Because the number of people is usually small, and because of prevailing consensus values, this aspect is crucial in rural community work.

There is a hesitancy among many rural people about setting in motion organised group activity.

Thus a worker's enabling and facilitating skills may have to be applied over a long time-period with only minimal results being apparent. Facilitating and enabling in direct community work is about judging the pace of a community and using encouragement judiciously.

(iv) *Organising* – once a worker is involved then it is likely that she will be supporting a number of different activities and groups. Accordingly, she will need good organising skills. It may be, for example, that in addition to working with people in one parish she is working across several parishes, and therefore having to handle the relationships between them.

We use the term 'organising' for the nuts-and-bolts work done by the community worker to form, build and maintain community groups. It includes the routines of attending meetings and helping groups plan and achieve tasks successfully. It also encompasses both campaign work by groups, and assisting their links with the various statutory and voluntary agencies. Accordingly the community worker has to be skilled at relating to a range of agencies, explaining the nature of her job to the appropriate officers and elected members, and finding ways of improving the work and services of agencies in the community where she is working. There is, we feel, an element of the worker using the go-between or brokerage skills in this kind of work, a point we develop later.

Indigenous workers

In outlining the core elements of direct community work we should not assume that the work will always be done by a practitioner from outside the community. Indeed, given the importance of the worker being part of the community, there is a strong case for agencies making use of indigenous community workers as part of their strategy. We have been excited by examples we have seen of local people taking on the role of community worker, and surprised by the limited recognition this dimension has received within rural community work. Accordingly, even though the number of people involved in this way will be small compared to professionals, we propose to illustrate its potential.

The term itself, indigenous or local community worker, refers to several potential roles. We identify three:

(i) *Community leader* – where the energy and vision of a local person lead him or her into playing the central role in an initiative. In a sense, he or she *is* the initiative; others follow where he or she goes first. This does not mean that the role is an autocratic one. Frequently the person concerned will be aware that the drive behind an initiative has been very dependent on him or her, and will seek to become more of a resource than a leader.

This was the intention of the community enterprise project set up by Berwyn Evans in the small village of Pentrefoelas on the Clwyd/ Gwynedd border of North Wales. A former businessman, Berwyn Evans had followed a European Commission-funded rural development course at a nearby college. From there he came back to Pentrefoelas and, while not actually re-settling in the village, played a lead role in reviving the village through a combination of tourism, handicrafts and the renovation of buildings. It relied upon the commitment and acumen of a handful of individuals. Exploiting the position of the village on a major tourist route, Berwyn Evans had the village's former public conveniences converted into a locally-controlled tourist information centre; on the other side of the road are shops, a cafe and a heritage trail.

The initiative avoided a 'go it alone' stance by drawing in the five neighbouring villages to the plans. It is a fascinating example of individual enterprise which yet is lodged within a strong sense of responsibility to the survival, culture and Welsh language of the local community; all three are deeply embedded in Pentrefoelas. Bailey and Scott (1989) comment that, 'The support he identifies that is required to sustain Welsh culture has little to do with imported technical/artistic inputs, but rather a major improvement in the local economy.'

Berwyn Evans used to the full outside advisors (especially from the Welsh Tourist Board) and the availability of various grants. He also worked closely with the local authorities. What the initiative has not had, however, is any external community work support. Berwyn Evans has taken the community worker role, in that it has been interwoven with an overt leadership position within the community. It illustrates well, therefore, the scope for this type of indigenous worker for practising direct community work.

(ii) *'Political' leader* – a role similar to that outlined above, and relying too on individual energy and charisma, but more closely aligned to political systems and networks. There are likely to be both traditional political systems, notably within local government, and networks which support, and advocate for, rural community work.

Our example again comes from Wales: the building-up of a flourishing, multi-purpose community centre outside Narberth in West Wales relied heavily on Joan Asby. Her involvement was over ten years. She had been a personnel officer and she drew on these skills in her community work. She became a county councillor and combined this with extending the centre both in terms of supporting community initiatives in surrounding villages and in linking the community and cultural functions of the centre to community economic initiatives such as small workspace units for local crafts.

The role of political leader is more high profile than that of a community leader. It relies upon public legitimacy and is more closely connected to political and community work networks. Within it, however, we can identify two essential attributes of a local community worker: a strong commitment to the social and economic development of a specified rural area, and the capacity and skills to undertake the day-by-day organising and contacting which is the bread and butter of community work.

(iii) *Experienced community worker* – a trained and experienced person who, having been employed as a community worker in other contexts, undertakes community work as a local resident, i.e. in an unpaid, voluntary capacity.

While one does not want to exaggerate the number of individuals or partners who are involved in this way, it is important to capture the role, not only because this may inform others in a similar position but also because there can be variations on the theme. Someone may be in full-time employment elsewhere, possibly unrelated to community work, or in the opposite situation: not employed at all, or working from home. The crucial ingredient is that the person is part of a community in his or her own right: hence the scope for genuinely understanding the feelings, aspirations, anxieties of friends and neighbours. Often this person will have returned to live in the community in which he or she was brought up.

The role provides considerable opportunities to residents who have a job or position in the community – the priest, the playgroup organiser, chairperson of the parish council, etc. There need be nothing underhand about such individuals taking on a community worker role. Taylor (1976) has noted that, 'A person... going about his usual work is likely to find greater acceptance within the village and have a strong basis from which to develop his community involvement.' The same would be true for those who have no obvious position or status in the community.

One of the people with whom we discussed this role took up the position of parish clerk. Jackie Denman had considerable experience of rural community work in Herefordshire prior to moving to an isolated hamlet in the county. In wanting to contribute to the social well-being of the community, she found that being parish clerk gave her a structure within which to do community work. She was active with the Women's Institute, the playgroup, and a festival. She found it useful to refer back to former colleagues and her previous employing agency – the rural community council:

> I can call on my past experience and inner strength, but some form of back-up is essential. This is because combining the roles of resident and community worker produces its own tensions. There is a danger, for instance, of over-using the information you acquire and of dominating. Sometimes you have to let things go by, lose the opportunity if you like. (Personal communication, 1989)

Jackie Denman's experience of working as a local community worker in this way has important lessons. Her observations of the interaction between women involved in community activities spring from informal contact, often taking place daily over a long period of time. She has also been able to show how conventional organisations like a parish council and a Women's Institute branch can change and take on new ideas, mostly as a result of patient work done by someone like herself.

The second example of direct community work being practised by an experienced local community worker is from Northern Ireland. In 1976 Niall Fitzduff returned to the community on Lough Neagh where he was brought up, and began a small woodworking business. He encouraged people to use the workshop, and set up woodwork classes. From this experience there developed an interest in local history and, with the encouragement of the WEA, speakers were invited – an old shed was renovated as a venue – and at the same time local people were encouraged to tell their own stories.

Other classes were organised, and they began to move out to other venues in the community. Niall Fitzduff was aware, however, that he continued to be looked to as the initiator:

That is fairly typical of what I think you will find happens in a rural community to the teacher, doctor and priest: roles become very fixed and it can take a long time to shift that leadership. However, that was a central objective of the level and way in which I was working. (N. Fitzduff, 1992)

We have described how this community worker began his involvement because it points to the advantages of beginning slowly and carefully to encourage communication and participation amongst rural people. On the trust and organisation established within the Lough Neagh community it was possible to build a major campaign against the activities of BP in drilling for lignite. Out of it came a community development project which, in addition to broadening the lignite campaign, was designed as an integrated rural development project, showing how a community can move into the future. A newspaper was launched. There was also a summer playscheme, Christmas party and the setting-up of a resource centre (see Henderson and Francis, 1992). Like the Herefordshire example, the experience of this community worker provides some remarkable insights into the nature of involvement in a close-knit, traditional rural community.

There are problems about confusion of roles for this kind of community worker, especially when he or she is moving through several different roles over a period of time. On a more practical note, there are problems about paying for telephone calls and postage. There may well be a case for trusts and other funding sources to be ready to support initiatives of such local workers on a small-scale, flexible basis.

The potential is exciting, not only because the local worker is acting so closely to the community but also because, as a result of previous experience, he or she can bring an outside perspective to local issues, thereby helping to show the extent to which many local problems are caused by powerful external economic and social forces. We are far from suggesting that there is potential in all rural communities for this kind of approach. It will depend on the availability of an competent community worker, and on the history, population and culture of any one community.

It seems to us that salaried professionals – community workers, social workers, clergy, youth workers – can learn important lessons for themselves from these experiences. What stands out is the importance of investing time and effort in genuinely understanding, and getting close to, the experiences and aspirations of rural people – an identification with communities, in which most professionals have not grown up but with which they seek to work. It is this argument which should underpin 'patch' and decentralisation strategies by social services departments and other agencies in rural areas.

Role

Inseparable from the community work role of someone practising direct community work is his or her lifestyle. There has to be congruence between the two. Problems will arise if a community worker is seeking to work within the cultural values of a community, but by his or her behaviour exhibits a quite different set of values. By lifestyle we mean behaviour which, because it is seen to be congruent with local culture and tradition, does not undermine the worker's objective of winning acceptance and of obtaining legitimacy. It is similar to the advice given by Von Hoffman (1972) to the good organiser: 'If you are a vegetarian, keep it to yourself, hide it, because there are a certain number of butchers in the community, and you want them in the organisation too.' Our advice does not seek to constrain the lives of community workers. Rather, it alerts him or her to the tendency of rural people not to separate the person and personal from the professional.

The ability of the community worker to take a non-directive role in direct community work will determine long-term effectiveness. We have here a contrast with the worker's directive role in focused, indirect work. Furthermore, we suggest that there is a close relationship between non-directiveness and process goals (see Rothman, 1969). The worker and his or her agency should both be profoundly interested in the long-term development of a community. We have argued that the worker has to get 'inside' a community to a far greater extent than in the other two strands of the model. It is from that vantage point that he or she takes on a strong developmental role, including making sure that the 'hidden' issues are addressed. Thus the argument for non-directiveness rests upon two closely connected themes: the pace at which rural communities can become organised and the long-term nature of direct community work. Between them they argue for the non-directive role of the worker.

In contrast to directiveness there is a considerable literature on non-directiveness (reviewed in Henderson and Thomas, 1987, pp. 108–12). Most trained community workers are predisposed to the role. In a sense, the contemporary practitioner has to update the language of non-directiveness developed by Batten (1967) and others who based their theories substantially on rural development programmes in developing countries. The key characteristic of the non-directive role is the ability to give local people the space to develop their plans and take decisions. The worker is there to support them in this:

> He does not provide answers; he has questions which stimulate insight. He does not carry the burden of responsibility for organising and action in the community; he provides encouragement and support for those who do. (Ross and Lappin, 1967)

This stance, with its emphasis on the activity of questioning, puts the worker in a definite, specifiable role. Non-directiveness calls for patience and self-discipline. The worker must be prepared to let a group develop in ways it decides, so that it is aware that is has power. Yet the worker's role is interventionist, he or she is not a detached onlooker. On the contrary, there is a need to show understanding of a group's problems and give encouragement at appropriate times. Above all, he or she must combine non-directiveness with demonstrable commitment to tasks and to groups. It is impossible in direct community work to have contact without commitment.

A broker?

We have found that many rural community workers based in localities take on the role of broker or go-between, especially between community groups and powerful agencies such as local authorities: they help to clarify and explain the positions or demands of different parties. One explanation for this is that community leaders are not there in sufficient numbers to do it. It is a role which, in the literature and amongst community workers, tends to be shunned: 'encourage representatives of a group to communicate directly with powerholders, do not try to do it on their behalf', has been the refrain. The rural experience is that such a rigid position is inadequate, albeit the long-term objective should be to encourage the people involved in a community initiative (not necessarily the identified leaders) to speak and act on their own behalf at all times.

The perceived neutral status of the rural community worker lends weight to the case for him or her to act at times as a go-between. In his assessment of the Waveney Project, Moseley draws attention to the advantage of the worker not having an axe to grind, and he links this to the need of the worker to have 'a scrupulous concern for communication – constantly going round the villages meeting people, explaining what he could (and could not) do, using the media, keeping people in touch' (Moseley, 1985).

Concluding comments

In her critique of rural community development in Britain, Susan Wright suggests that it is among community workers like the one with the Wyeside project that there is most likely to be an awareness of conflicts of interests in communities. The advantage of working intensively, over a period of time, is that opportunities emerge to support those people who do not belong to existing organisations or established networks:

> There is a cumulative change in the individuals' value of themselves, but this is achieved almost in spite of the system through which they were made invisible and unheard in the first place. (Wright, 1990)

Bringing about change in this fundamental sense probably provides the strongest argument for resourcing the direct community work strand of rural community work. Ultimately, the approach is one which seeks to empower people who otherwise are excluded from participating in rural society. It does so through its commitment to the idea of process – how things happen as well as what happens – and its capacity to facilitate and sustain it. This, as we have seen, may require a long time-scale in most rural contexts.

That is why the question of management and support is of critical importance for direct community work practice, and we address this in the following chapter.

8

Management in Rural Community Work

Introduction

'We are very happy with our patchworker. I have little idea what she does, but she seems to get results, and communities like her.'

'What I most like about my job is the freedom. I can get on with what I want without any interference, and know that people appreciate what I'm doing.'

'On the whole, we have had a good year in this county. Two village hall committees managed to build new halls, and several more undertook major renovation projects. We held three major conferences for parish councils: on rural housing, planning and community care. The number of entries was up on previous years for our Best Kept Village Competition. And we ended the year with a slight financial surplus.'

These three statements are paraphrased from the extensive interviews which we conducted with rural community work people throughout the UK. The first quote came from a manager of a small voluntary agency, who had to fit his management and administrative work around his own direct fieldwork responsibilities. The second one came from an out-posted patch community worker, who had been doing the job for about two years, and who had had no previous community work experience. The third came from the introduction to the annual report of a county-wide voluntary agency.

We see management as a crucial tool in making rural community work practice effective, and in attaining the higher practice standards which are increasingly demanded in rural community work.

115

'Management' is a word covering a multitude of purposes, roles and tasks. Our experience of most rural agencies is that these various aspects of management are not addressed in a clear-cut, traditionally hierarchical way. It is not uncommon, as in any small organisation, to find that the field community work staff also have 'management' responsibilities, and that the managers also have fieldwork responsibilities. As an example of this latter point, our survey of community workers in the UK (Francis *et al.*, 1984) showed that over half the directors of English and Welsh rural community councils saw themselves as practitioners of community work, rather than purely as managers.

The management of an agency or project requires a number of functions: the supervision, appraisal and development of staff; financial management; personnel management; public relations and liaison; planning; programme management; evaluation. Many of the tasks, skills and knowledge required for each of these functions are common to the management of any agency or project, and are not unique to rural community work practice. In this chapter, we deliberately focus on two aspects of management: the support of community work staff, and the evaluation of community work.

We noted in Chapter 3 that there is resistance among many rural community workers and their agencies to the adoption of a strategic approach to their work. It is probably not surprising that that same resistance which applies to the planning of the work is also prevalent in its operational management. Management and evaluation, and the support and development of workers, are either given a low priority, or they are rejected as contrary to the ethos of the job. These views, however regrettable, should not be dismissed as dogmatic conservatism, as there are some very good, tangible explanations, many of which are well documented in the community work literature. For example, the research by Thomas and Warburton (1977) into community workers in a social services department found that:

—— supervisors or managers are often not experienced in, or knowledgeable about, community work and so are not in a good position to offer informed comment or help to their workers

—— time is precious to community work staff and managers, and is better spent on development work in the field than on internal matters

—— community workers do not record their activities and observations in sufficient detail, and managers are not able to any great extent to see their workers in action out in the field, so that it is difficult to expect any informed comment
—— community workers value their independence, and resent interference by managers
—— as there is no clear consensus as to the terms of reference and methods of community work, the management process cannot productively prescribe 'right' ways and reject 'wrong' ways

Similar fears are expressed by managers and fieldworkers about evaluation. It is perceived as a threat to the harmony and independence of community work. It is often felt to be a strain on precious resources of time and money. Especially when undertaken by 'outsiders', it is frequently dismissed as missing the point about what community work is *really* about, by concentrating on those aspects which are the most tangible.

While we agree that these arguments can present difficulties, they are *relative* constraints, against which must be set the advantages of staff management and evaluation:

—— to ensure good planning and the setting of clear objectives and sensible work programmes
—— to ensure that strategies and programmes actually do get carried out
—— to ensure that resources (including staff) are brought into play, to enable the programme to succeed
—— to keep the worker in touch with developments and trends in the agency and wider world
—— to keep the agency in touch with what is happening on the ground, so that it can adjust its policies and programmes where necessary
—— to maintain the worker's morale and confidence, and help with problem-solving
—— to improve the worker's competence, effectiveness and career development
—— to ensure that communities receive help which is appropriate
—— to improve the agency's performance

In other words, despite some practical difficulties, there are good reasons why community work agencies and fieldworkers, however hard pressed they are in vast rural areas, should devote some time to management and evaluation.

Staff management

The support and guidance of community work staff is important for three reasons:

—— community work staff are probably the most important element in community work practice
—— staff supervision and appraisal requires an understanding of the practice of rural community work, which is less necessary for other aspects of management such as financial or personnel management
—— our research revealed a widespread shortage of good staff management practice in rural community work

We believe that the ethos of community work should be reflected within the community work agency. Therefore, it is probably more helpful to talk about the supervision and appraisal of staff performance, rather than staff management, which may have connotations of control and the exercise of power. Supervision and appraisal are not a single function with a single objective, and so it should not be assumed that responsibility for these tasks can necessarily fall on the shoulders of just one person. To help identify the various facets of supervision and appraisal, Thomas and Warburton (1977), drawing on earlier writings by other authors, identified three main functions:

Administrative functions involve a concern with work assignment and planning; review, monitoring and evaluation; co-ordinating, facilitating and sanctioning work; channelling communication and policy formulation and community liaison.

Supportive functions involve a responsibility to sustain worker morale, helping overcome job-related discouragements and discontents, giving supervisees a sense of worth as professionals, a sense of belonging in the agency and a sense of security in their performance.

Educational functions involve developing the knowledge and the skills of the worker, improving the level of competence with which she or he thinks about and does the work – including evaluation and self-evaluation.

Each of these functions calls for its own set of tasks, skills and knowledge. Some of them, notably the 'administrative' functions, are quite clearly and traditionally in the province of 'the manager'. Others, notably the educational functions, may well be addressed more effectively through other channels, which we shall look at later in this chapter.

One example of how this typology may be turned into practice is given by Ann Meadows who, on behalf of ACRE, addressed the staff management and development needs of English rural community councils. She has stressed the need for both managerial supervision and for non-managerial or professional development supervision.

Managerial supervision concerns the contractual relationship between the supervisor and employee. To ensure that the work gets done, the employee agrees to carry out certain duties, for which the supervisor undertakes to provide the necessary resources, which could include finance, support, information. Both the supervisor and the worker have their own agendas for the supervision, and the process is, in effect, a form of negotiation. It is not simply the supervisor telling the worker what to do, and finding out whether the last lot of work has been carried out. It obviously embraces the administrative functions of supervision, but it must also fulfil some of the supportive and educational functions. That is, beyond negotiations of what will and will not get done, managerial supervision must address the worker's practical and emotional needs: for example, helping them to foresee and overcome practical difficulties, promoting a sense of pride and value in their work, boosting their morale.

Professional development supervision is concerned with enhancing the competence of the worker. The agenda is set by the worker, who brings whatever concerns, case material etc. she or he wishes the supervision process to address. There is a large emphasis on questions of 'how' and 'why', and on the development of skills. The supervisor's main contribution is professional expertise, and his or her role is not one of ensuring that work gets done. The supervisor may have to adopt a long-term perspective in reviewing the development of the worker's performance and approach over a number of sessions. Professional development supervision is largely concerned with the educational function, but it clearly also addresses the supportive function and it facilitates the administrative function.

These two supervision processes tend to have a short-term focus, and supervision sessions should ideally occur every month or so. In addition to supervision, the third type of support and development is provided by *staff performance appraisal*, concerned with the longer-term perspective of a worker's accomplishments, performance, outlook and career development. It is concerned with supportive and educational functions, rather than with the planning and implementation of work. It requires careful structuring and handling, and it need take place no more than once or twice a year.

It is important to stress that the two types of supervision, and appraisal, are not alternative forms of staff management: they are all necessary, and complementary to each other, in addressing the needs of the worker, the agency and the constituency. Each process has a different role, and calls for special skills, knowledge and attitudes on the part of the 'manager'.

Managerial supervision calls for something more than general management skills, an understanding of a strategy and work programme, and a commitment to seeing it carried out. The supervisor needs to be aware of and sensitive to the realities of community work practice and of rural communities. This is important not only to ensure that agreed programmes of work are viable and realistic, but also to help the worker to gain a better understanding of his or her tasks and an appreciation of the value of the work and his or her own contribution to it.

This kind of understanding is usually present, to varying degrees, when the supervisor has 'come up through the ranks' of doing community work, but not when someone has come to the job from a quite different background. In our research, we found little evidence of a career progression within rural community work, so that many managers come from non-community work and non-rural backgrounds. Especially in the first few years, they are probably more in the dark about the realities of practice than the fieldworkers whom they are supervising. While they may bring some useful contributions to the supervision process, such as a sympathetic ear and experience of life, it is likely that unless they take steps to learn fast they will not be able to do full justice to the managerial supervision process.

Professional development supervision calls for a different role, a different relationship between supervisor and worker and different (though overlapping) skills on the part of the supervisor. These can be very good reasons for finding a different supervisor for this purpose and possibly someone who is outside the organisation. It is a role that calls for counselling and training skills, for a good knowledge of rural community work and for a high degree of trust and confidentiality in what can be a very personal relationship between supervisor and worker. More than in managerial supervision, the professional development supervisor needs to be closely matched to the needs and personality of the worker. In small agencies the provision of this sort of supervision is rare, partly because of the resource implications (it will almost always be given a lower priority than managerial supervision) and because the right combination of supervisor and worker is hard to find. In rural areas, where 'social practitioners' of any sort are thin on the ground, it would be unusual to find a professional development supervisor with all the right attributes to match a rural community worker.

Realities of practice

What we have been talking about so far is the mixture of general concepts about management, which could apply to a range of activities and scales of agency. They have been drawn largely from the literature. In order to ground these theories in the real world of rural community work, we need to address the factors and issues which might constrain and influence its application.

For many rural community workers, the realities of their work are that they are involved in a practice in which they have little prior experience or training; they are working in complex and sophisticated social systems, and alongside other complex agencies; they are often isolated, whether geographically or organisationally, from the management centre of their agency; they often operate with impossibly vague or open terms of reference with little guidance over priorities; they are often so immersed in their work, working way beyond their contracted hours, that they have little time or energy to create their own systems of support; and their managers, however well-intentioned, have neither sufficient time nor understanding to give the full support that may be needed. It is very likely that their needs will alter, over time, and therefore the management response should similarly adjust.

In their early months as a rural community worker, just about everything is new to them: the agency and wider environment and the nature of the work. For some, the environment may be a little familiar to them, if they come from a rural background and/or have received an education with a strong rural flavour; however, the work, their role and their work environment, they may be experiencing for the first time. For some others, a background in youth or social work may have prepared them for some aspects of the work but the rural situation in all its complexities may be quite new.

A year or so into the job, the worker will have some grasp of the work and some understanding about the constituency, the people and the issues. The attainment of some successes in the field (for example, the establishment of a community newsletter or pre-school playgroup) may be sufficient reassurance and motivation to satisfy the worker, the agency and the communities that she or he is doing a good job. The worker has moved from a position of confusion and helplessness to one of satisfaction, supported by a sense of freedom and independence.

Several years into the job, the earlier euphoria begins to wear off. The worker becomes aware that the communities with which she or he is working are complex, with gainers and losers, unequally competing factions, non-joiners, people who seem superficially well-off but who in other ways are disadvantaged. She or he also becomes more aware that there are choices to be made about which issues to tackle, in which communities, with which techniques, including which people, for which ultimate end, etc. At the same time, the agency and its funders may be demanding visible results. They may also be expressing concern about what they regard as the 'embarrassments' which some of the work is causing, and the communities themselves are also becoming more demanding of the worker as well as of the authorities. The 'honeymoon period' is over and the job is presenting some very real demands, not only on the worker's time but also on his or her range of skills, knowledge, faculties, and professional sense of well-being.

Of course, this general picture of a rural community worker's development over a period of time is artificial, but it illustrates the point that the management needs of a rural community worker do evolve, and it is important to gear the management approach to the needs of the worker. One manifestation of this is in a four-stage effective leadership model, based upon the worker's development in the job:

(i) *The person is new to the job.* They need a great deal of guidance, but they also need time to try their hand at the work. The manager therefore provides specific instructions, and pays close attention to what the worker does.

(ii) *The worker is gaining in experience.* The required tasks cannot just be specified: they need to be explained to the worker who may wish clarification and discussion of the work. It is no longer enough to tell the worker what to do: motivation and persuasion is also necessary, as the worker gains in confidence and critical awareness.

(iii) *The worker is now settled into the job, and more confident and competent.* Instead of the manager deciding what work should be done, it is now a matter of participation and discussion: sharing ideas and collaborating. The provision of encouragement and support to the worker is important.

(iv) *The worker is now well established, with a high degree of confidence and competence.* It is both practicable and desirable to give the worker responsibility for decision-making and implementation in his or her area of work. There is a high degree of 'delegated power', but it is still important for the manager to monitor the work, and not to abdicate responsibility and interest.

The rate of progress during these stages, together with the subtleties of supervision within any one of them, is a matter of judgement and skill, but it must relate to the ability and willingness of the worker to progress. For different workers in the same agency, a different level of management may be called for, and this may also apply to different areas of work undertaken by the same worker.

However, we believe that the management response which is appropriate at different stages of a rural community worker's job requires something more than the degree of responsibility which they are permitted. It is a complex interplay of familiarisation, training, acquisition of values and knowledge, sensitising, motivation, intellectual challenge, rewards, questioning and regeneration. It must derive from an understanding of a worker's needs and situation, and a willingness to do something to meet them.

The management response must not only be appropriate to the worker's life-cycle in the job, but also to the nature of the work itself. Here, our three-track model of rural community work is important, as we believe that the three tracks require different supervision or support. The detail of that supervision will be readily apparent from our earlier coverage of these three ways of working and we do not intend to spell them out again here. However, the general point we wish to make is that the supervisor must be familiar with the methods in which the worker is engaging, if she or he is to be in a position to help the worker to be effective and to overcome the inherent pitfalls in the methods being used. Therefore, the nature of the supervisor's skill and knowledge – the goods that they can deliver – must be relevant to the worker's practice which, in an agency or project with workers adopting different approaches to their work, may require a wide and diverse range of attributes on the part of the supervisor.

The realities are that supervisors very often do not have time to do justice to these needs, some are quite probably not sufficiently interested in their workers' practice, some workers (particularly those who are out-posted and/or work part-time) cannot easily get access to their supervisors and, as we outlined at the beginning, supervision in community work in general is faced with difficulties. It is therefore important for community workers to explore and develop additional systems of support to meet their needs. Networking, linking with other similar workers to provide mutual support, can help to contribute to the professional development aspects of supervision. This may be achieved through a group approach, or by pairing, i.e. two workers supporting each other. The report on courses held in the Derbyshire Rural Development Area (Andrews, 1988) is a helpful example of such an initiative. Training is almost certainly required, to help the workers to help each other. Compatibility of personality, intellect and values is an important consideration here: it is arguably more important for the partner to be 'on the same wavelength' than to be fully conversant with the detail of one's practice.

Evaluation

Evaluation is an important and integral part of the management of rural community work, and should not be regarded as an optional extra which can be 'bolted-on' to the end of a project, or discarded, according to whether people have the time and motivation. Especially since the late 1980s community work, along with many other activities, has been under increasing pressure to involve systems of evaluation. This desire for more rigorous evaluation has been accompanied by the UK government's concern to secure the three E's: economy, effectiveness and efficiency, in its own activities and in the programmes which it has funded.

Evaluation is not a single process, but rather a range of tools for showing people how an agency, group, person or programme is doing. It gives answers to questions such as: 'are we accomplishing what we set out to do?', 'just how successful have our efforts been?', 'have we made the best use of our limited resources?', 'was that project really the big failure which people said it was?'.

Evaluation does not have to be a mystical process, it does not have to be particularly sophisticated, and it does not have to be a threat. Evaluation can be very useful in helping agencies and individuals to improve their performance: to build upon their successes and to learn from mistakes. It can also be an effective way of communicating to other bodies, including funders, those in positions of power, and local people, just what a programme or type of work is really about. It is not only the contents of an evaluation which can be persuasive. The very fact that an evaluation is being undertaken can put out reassuring signals that the agency or individual worker is organised and conscientious.

However, 'evaluation' is, with some justification, not always viewed in such a positive way. It can also be seen as:

—— a *threat*: especially when it is imposed by an outside powerful body, with possible fears of cutbacks in funding, job redundancies, an enforced, unwelcome change of direction, or an undermining of the self-respect and harmony of the staff team

—— a *drain on resources*: the time or money spent on evaluation uses resources which might otherwise be spent on direct practical action. This is particularly resented where evaluation is viewed as an encumbrance, external to the planning, management and delivery of community work

—— *irrelevant*: evaluation is more frequently accused of being irrelevant or superfluous when it is carried out by people from outside the agency. They can be criticised for 'missing the point', for failing to capture the essence of what the agency or piece of work is really about, or for undermining the whole purpose of a programme by focusing on the 'wrong' set of objectives or values

Therefore, the positive virtues of evaluation are under pressure from negative considerations. Rural community work all too often opts for the line of least resistance by emphasising the difficulties, concluding that the evaluation is a desirable but not essential management activity. This outlook is not particularly surprising for a discipline which traditionally has been more comfortable with 'practical doing' than with thinking about the practice.

Progress is impeded by the relative shortage of good evaluative materials (processes, reports, training courses, etc.), from which practitioners can learn and develop. This is partly due to a failure of rural community work to be clear about its objectives and values (what is it really trying to do, and what does it believe in?), but also due to the greater difficulties in assessing soft and qualitative processes concerned with the development of people, compared with the measurement of hard, tangible outputs and results. Finally, there is the problem inherent in any community work intervention: objectives change as a result of a group's decision to make a change in direction, and the community worker has to adjust his or her work accordingly. This means that measuring the impact of community work can be very difficult.

We do not believe that the above reservations constitute a fundamental obstacle. Instead, they provide a challenge to us to evolve a clearer understanding of what evaluation means (and what it can and cannot do) and to evolve a choice of methods which are appropriate to rural community work practice. A major part of this process is to de-mystify the whole concept of evaluation.

Evaluation is the collection and processing of information relating to the performance and results of a programme, activity or system, followed by an assessment or value-judgement of these matters, to arrive at some conclusions. These conclusions should then be used to confirm, abandon or modify the work.

Evaluation is therefore something more than monitoring, which is a process of collecting and recording information, without drawing any conclusions about success, failure, value or worthlessness. Monitoring may pick up on what is happening in a variety of sectors:

—— *the locality*: for example seasonal unemployment may be increasing, a new youth club is started, a new housing estate is built

—— *other agencies*: the worker or agency is not an island, and it is important to know, for example, what new policies are emerging from the local authorities, what new laws are affecting a parish council's powers, or what public services are being cut back

—— *the worker's agency*: it is important to know how many, and which, community groups are receiving help, how many people are receiving and reading the newsletter or how quickly the worker is responding to requests for help

Monitoring is relatively value-free. It tells people what is happening but it does not pass judgement on this, or on whether there are better ways of organising the work. Both monitoring and evaluation are important components in community work, but only evaluation tells us something about value and worth.

Planning and organising evaluation

There is no specifically rural dimension to evaluation. The principles are the same whatever the environment, although the prevalence of smaller, under-resourced agencies and out-posted workers in rural areas probably points towards the need for low-cost and informal evaluation techniques more than formal and sophisticated processes.

There are several good texts available on the role and processes of evaluation in activities which are orientated towards people (community work, social work, the voluntary sector, etc.): for example, Key, Hudson and Armstrong (1976); Feek and Smith (1984); Hedley (1985); Ball (1988); Meadows and Turkie (1988); Feek (1988); Feuerstein (1986); Oakley (1988).

These writings see the shortcomings of the sort of evaluation which is preoccupied with the easy-to-measure, 'hard-line' data such as counting the number of community projects which have been created, or assessing the financial cost of a particular programme. These techniques, even if they manage to progress beyond a monitoring or audit process to some kind of value-based assessment, generally fail to address the softer, developmental outcomes of rural community work: for example, people's preparedness to work together, a community's ability to anticipate and manage change, confidence and a sense of competence amongst disadvantaged people. They also tend to focus on results, and ignore the equally important aspects of *processes*.

Ian Morrison (1989) of Westhill College, Birmingham University, has stressed the importance of process to community work and therefore of the need to evaluate the work itself and not just the outcomes. In his briefing pack he points to eight key indicators which an evaluation of the process of community work should look for. They include:

—— participation (i.e. becoming involved in influencing things)
—— voluntarism (choosing of one's own free will to get involved)
—— mutuality (sharing the recognition, appreciation and support of each other)
—— holistic (seeing people in a complete sense, and not just in a single role or category)

—— diversity (creating a choice of opportunities for participation, in different ways and at different levels)
—— relationships (the emergence and development of friendly, effective and constructive relationships)
—— challenge (stretching people to achieve more, beyond their limited horizons)
—— fun (bringing pleasure into the process)

A number of questions have to be asked and answered before deciding upon an appropriate evaluation strategy:

(i) *Why evaluate?* In the introduction to this part of the chapter, we looked at the benefits and the concerns. It is a question which needs to be addressed by various different parties (practitioners, managers, funders, communities, etc.) and some discussion and negotiation may be needed to try and reconcile any differences in objectives.

(ii) *For whom is the evaluation being planned?* The scope and nature of the evaluation will greatly depend on this, and it should not be assumed that all audiences and needs can be satisfied by the same evaluation process or product. They may need different information, or a different form of presentation. For example, a project's staff who are wanting to improve their performance may need a great deal of material giving insight into how they work with one another, or into how their values and personality appear to affect their relationship with community groups. This kind of material is best kept restricted to this limited audience, and will be of little interest to funding agencies. The latter may be more interested, for example, in whether the community work approach is more effective than some other form of intervention in achieving specific goals.

(iii) *Who should carry out the evaluation?* This is only partly a question of resources (i.e. can we afford to pay an external evaluator; do we have time to do the job ourselves?). It also raises questions about power relationships, about who 'owns' the evaluation, about the acceptability or bias implicit in the findings, about the commitment of the people who need to be involved to provide full and honest information. An outside evaluator *may* be able to bring experience, impartiality, greater legitimacy and credibility, and an ability to draw informed comparisons with agencies or programmes elsewhere, but the down-side is that an outside evaluator may bring an inappropriate externally determined agenda and methodology; she or he may be insensitive and demanding of staff and of local communities, who ultimately feel no particular commitment to accepting and implementing the findings of the evaluation.

In addition to the questions surrounding who should be in charge of the evaluation are the further ones of who else should be involved and in what ways. In trying to answer this, one is immediately caught up in a classic and more general dilemma of community work: that of 'should the wider community be involved in the process, or in the interests of efficiency is it better not to?' If evaluation is a time-consuming exercise, then it will be much more so if some level of community involvement is necessary, and yet community workers could be accused of sacrificing their own principles if they fail to do so.

(iv) *What should be evaluated?* This question needs to be addressed at several levels:

—— should it be the whole strategy, or particular programmes or pieces of work within the strategy?

—— should it focus on the obvious quantifiable and more widely accepted aspects of rural community work (such as village services provided and/or saved), or should it also try to embrace the softer, less tangible matters (such as changed attitudes, and levels of confidence)?

—— should it look at processes, as well as the 'products on the ground'?

(v) *When should the evaluation be done?* Evaluation should be planned from the start of a piece of work, and not be left as an afterthought to be addressed, if time and resources permit, at the end. Evaluation should run concurrently with the implementation of a piece of work or a strategy. It should be noted that the process of evaluation can be modest and relatively informal. It does not have to be a highly resourced, once-and-for-all event, which would be particularly inappropriate during the early life of a project.

(vi) *How should the evaluation be done?* A wide variety of techniques are possible, including the following which have been listed by Key *et al.* (1976):

—— *goal models*: assessing whether, and to what extent, the programme achieved its stated aims and objectives

———   *systems models*: assessing the extent to which the programme
has changed the outside world, with the use of a systems
model of the locality

———   *impressionistic enquiry*: the evaluator builds up a picture of
the project by sitting-in on meetings in the agency and the
community, by reading relevant reports, and by talking to
staff

———   *opinion surveys*: asking people for their knowledge and views
about a programme

———   *blue ribbon committees* and grateful testimonials: whereby
local dignitaries and/or people involved in community
groups produce statements usually praising the value of a
piece of work

———   *textbook precepts*: comparing the methods and activities of a
programme with 'textbook' examples of good practice.

Implications for practice

Evaluation of rural community work in the UK is relatively under-
developed, and this concluding section is therefore tentative rather
than based upon a variety of good, working examples. Rather than
providing a coherent model of how it could or should be done, we
identify a series of issues and practical tips for people to think
about:

(i) *Evaluation need not be comprehensive.* It is neither practicable
nor particularly necessary to attempt a full evaluation of all aspects
of an agency's work, all of the time. It would be more efficient and
effective to focus on a smaller range of topics: perhaps a case study
of the agency's work in one particular typical village community, to
assess and show how effective (or ineffective) the work has been; or
a constructively critical report commissioned from an outside, but
related, agency about the perceived strengths and weaknesses of
one's project; or a fuller appraisal of just one strand of the agency's
activity, such as its village halls advisory service or its volunteer
training programme.

On some occasions, the evaluation may be primarily soft or
subjective; on others, it may be more objective or based upon hard
indicators. Over a period of time, different pieces of work, or
different ways of looking at the agency's work can be considered,
building up gradually to a fuller overall picture.

(ii) *Evaluation and appropriateness.* We have argued that the different major strands of rural community work (working from a distance, focused indirect work and direct work) require different combinations of skills, knowledge, roles, etc. The nature and content of evaluation is also likely to differ, although not necessarily fundamentally. It will be harder to measure outcomes when working from a distance: the worker or agency may, in any year, 'sow a great many seeds', give numerous one-off pieces of advice and disseminate countless leaflets, briefing notes, newsletters, etc., but it is extremely difficult to identify the results of all of this work, and it is even more difficult to prove a causal link with these interventions.

Direct community work will – or should – be able to demonstrate not only the 'hard-line' outcomes (such as new village halls being built, a youth club with a wider curriculum and a firmer financial base or the retention of a rail service which had been threatened with closure) but also soft-line outcomes concerned with the health and vitality of the community. It may be less easy to identify these latter aspects, but relevant indicators may include:

—— the degree to which a community group is anticipating and influencing change, rather than belatedly reacting to it

—— whether people on the margins (socially, as well as geographically) are welcomed and are involved in community activities

—— the extent to which responsibility and decision-making is shared around the community.

Direct community work should also be in a better position to analyse the effect of its processes on what is happening within the group or community and Ian Morrison's process-related indicators which we outlined earlier are one way of addressing this issue.

However, while it is hoped that these indicative processes may happen within the community, whatever the community work approach, it will rarely be possible for the 'working from a distance' approach to be in a position to 'measure' them, and in the 'focused, indirect' approach it may be possible to gain only a superficial impression.

For the evaluation of any rural community work approach, it will be important to assess a combination of both quantitative and qualitative aspects, although we recognise the greater difficulty of gathering and appraising evaluation information relating to the outcomes and the processes involved in the less-local forms of community work. Nevertheless, it should still be possible on occasions for community workers to test out the efficacy of their methods in a variety of ways: by asking for (and seeking out) consumer reactions, by applying what could best be described as 'critical common sense', by making efforts to gauge the views of those communities or groups which do not use the agency's services. Much of the material may be impressionistic and anecdotal, but it will be as valid as data collected or measured in purportedly 'scientific' ways.

(iii) *Evaluation is everybody's responsibility.* Although evaluation is a key function in management, it should not be something which is only the concern of the official managers. Rural community workers need to be self-evaluators, especially so where they are out-posted or otherwise isolated from the rest of the agency. However, this should not always be an individual's responsibility: opportunities should be created for workers (whether or not from within the same agency) to meet, to discuss critically, and reflect upon their practice. It requires an agenda which extends beyond questions of 'what are you doing?' to the probing of 'how and why are you doing it?'.

Consumer reaction is important. Rural community workers should be encouraging communities to be critically aware of the world around them, and part of this process should involve communities articulating just what resources – including community work interventions – they require. Rural communities should not be content simply to 'make do' and accept passively whatever help a community worker chooses to give them. However, the relative inexperience of most communities in this respect makes us feel that the idea will not come easily, and the workers themselves must take purposeful steps to encourage the communities to be constructively critical of the worker's and agency's practice.

(iv) *Evaluation should be comfortable.* Whichever techniques are used, the processes of collecting and recording information, of discussing ideas and alternative viewpoints, of reaching conclusions and implementing them as a result, need to 'fit in' with the style and practices of the agency and its workers. Writers on community work often distinguish between two styles of behaviour adopted by agencies or individual workers: rational and intuitive. Rational behaviour is based upon systematic research, explicit planning, logical analysis, and what might be termed a bureaucratic (not in a negative sense) approach to administration.

Evaluation under this regime will be more amenable to a systematic and paper-based approach than under an intuitive regime, where qualities such as insight, spontaneity, revelation and empathy have a higher value. In practice, we believe that effective rural community work involves a combination of rational and intuitive behaviour, and appropriate evaluation techniques need to embody both: not only in the criteria which are used to gauge success, but also in the methods used to collect evaluative information and arrive at judgements.

In concluding this chapter, it is clear that community workers and their agencies have choices to make in finding appropriate management methods. The challenge is to develop the range of possibilities into a coherent process which matches the various management needs with the resources and style of the agency.

One example of how to achieve this is the staff development process which a regional community education service adopted in Scotland in the late 1980s:

Recruitment and interview:	a rigorous procedure involving accurate job descriptions and specifications
Induction:	a planned and high quality process
Work plan:	prepared by each community worker, and outlining the work for the next six months
Supervision:	to maintain work standards and minimise the risk of the unexpected
Training:	to renew and develop workers' skills
Appraisal and review:	evaluating the worker's practice and agreeing ways of achieving progress
Career development:	including rejuvenation, broadening experience, evolving new job descriptions.

(Borders Regional Council, Community Education Service, 1989)

The essential point about management is that it should not only be concerned with past and present practice but also have an eye to the future. Learning about what we have done, and what we are doing, should be built into the planning process to develop future practice. This is the theme of our final chapter.

9

Rural Community Work in the 1990s

In this final chapter we focus on the prospects for rural community work in the 1990s and beyond. We begin by reviewing initiatives which have been important to the development of rural community work practice. Then, we try to identify some of the key trends which might affect rural areas, before pointing to the challenges facing community work practice.

Historical perspective

We can trace the history of rural community work back at least as far as the 1920s, when there was a blossoming of rural community-related initiatives, notably in England. This was the era when the National Council of Social Service's Rural Department and the first rural community councils were formed: a time of village hall building, Women's Institute formation, land resettlement and a marked change in the rural social order as many country estates were sold off, and farmers began to replace the landed gentry as local community leaders. Paradoxically, this was also the time of the biggest agricultural depression in British history, when farmers went out of business, farm buildings, fields and woodlands fell into decay, landlords waived farm rents altogether just to ensure that the land continued to be maintained, and villages were, for many people, places of extreme poverty (Brasnett, 1969).

The central importance of resource availability to rural community work and to community-based initiatives was clear, and the history of this practice can be closely linked to the funding and

135

development policies of key national agencies, notably the Development Commission, the Carnegie UK Trust and the National Council of Social Service. Thus, for example, in many counties it is possible to identify the growth and subsequent early decline of rural community work activities with the Carnegie grants to RCCs of the 1920s, which came to an end in the early 1930s, and a renaissance of this activity in the early 1950s, linked to an agreement by the Development Commission to provide stable long-term funding for RCCs. Similarly in Scotland, the substantial increase in community work activity within the community education system can be linked to the Alexander Report (1975), and in Northern Ireland the modest introduction of paid rural community workers from the late 1970s derived from the Moyle Report (1975) and the provision of funds to enable district councils to employ community services officers. In the Republic of Ireland the establishment of the 50-year-old Muintir na Tire and the tradition of rural co-operatives provided a significant context for subsequent developments – see O'Donohue (1990) who argues that, since the decline of Muintir na Tire, 'there has not been any significant progress towards establishing a rural community movement'.

The 1970s marked a turning point in rural community work practice. Prior to this, practice had largely been the co-ordination and joint planning of voluntary action and service provision for rural areas, and providing support for specific aspects of community activity such as village hall building, adult education and music and drama activities. Following the new national interest in neighbourhood-based community work in urban areas, and influenced by proposals for rural projects, the Development Commission began to fund new workers with a specific community brief: that is, an expectation to work directly with and for specific communities. At this time, we can point to a small catalogue of significant initiatives:

—— Three short-lived feasibility studies in the early 1970s, looking at the community work needs of less remote rural areas which were experiencing urban growth pressures. The three areas were West Cumbria, North Hampshire, and Gwent/Monmouthshire. All three studies revealed the need to employ community workers to encourage the self-help provision of services, help to improve the work of parish councils and public participation in decision-making, and foster better links between public agencies and communities.

—— The establishment in 1973 of the Community Initiatives in the Countryside scheme, which funded the employment of county-wide community workers in most English and Welsh counties.

—— In the late 1970s, six local development/research initiatives were launched by RCCs, local authorities and the Dartington Amenity Research Trust in remoter rural parts of England, which focused on parts of Cornwall, Devon, Herefordshire, Shropshire, Staffordshire and Norfolk. Some of these remained as research only, but it is significant that several did spawn the early so-called 'patch-work' community projects including Wyeside (Herefordshire) and Staffordshire Moorlands.

—— In Scotland, there was a marked growth in statutory community education and social work during the 1970s, and a modest growth of community work through voluntary organisations, notably the district-level councils of social service.

—— In Northern Ireland, we have noted the introduction of district council community services officers in some rural areas. There was also some support for rural community work through the appointment of education and social workers with a 'community' brief by the area Boards, and a development of outreach work through the Northern Ireland Council of Social Services' Community Information Service.

The 1980s saw a host of initiatives, many of only short-lived significance but some which will have a more lasting impact. One of the most significant features in the UK was the impact of the economic recession, linked with a distinctive anti-state bias by the Conservative government. This had all sorts of implications for rural areas and community work:

—— Cutbacks in public services hit the rural areas particularly hard, due to their geographical and economic marginality. Primary schools and cottage hospitals closed, people-intensive services (such as field social work) were cut back and council house building was severely reduced.

—— Greater emphasis was placed on the role of the voluntary sector and individual self-help, but usually without any new resources to make it happen.

—— Local authorities had their resources and powers curtailed, which meant that they were less well placed to facilitate action by rural communities.

—— For the first time in decades, even apparently well-off rural areas were hit by unemployment and other deprivation, and agriculture became a much less prosperous activity.

There were significant advances in the 1980s on the wider rural front with the formation of national rural lobbies, of varying effectiveness, in England (Rural Voice, 1981), Scotland (Rural Forum, 1982), the Northern Ireland Rural Association (1984) and Rural Wales (1988). With the possible exception of the NIRA, these federations have been policy-orientated rural lobbies, with little specific community work focus. However, there was some progress on this front in the 1980s: for example, the establishment of ACRE, Action with Communities in Rural England, with a brief which included the promotion and development of rural community work practice; and the EEC-sponsored Northern Ireland Rural Action Project, which conducted well-constructed local fieldwork projects focusing on rural women, low-income farmers, welfare rights advice, community enterprise and service integration. The EEC itself began to show an interest in rural areas, beyond their role in agriculture, forestry and fishing, but the Commission arguably had little impact on many social aspects of UK rural life during the 1980s.

The link between rural community work practice and policies and programmes concerned with rural development is crucial. Both interventions exist to varying degrees in different parts of the UK, but it is questionable whether there were very many good examples of effective links being made at local level. Thus, for example, the Northern Ireland Rural Action Project was a well-conceived rural community work scheme which was forced to operate in a near vacuum of rural policy due to the disinterest of government departments and boards. In many parts of Scotland, good community work was being undertaken, but with little relationship to policies and programmes aimed at rural development. In England, the mid-1980s saw the launch of Rural Development Programmes in most of the peripheral areas of the country. However, with one or two exceptions, there has been little room for community work or local involvement in the development of appropriate rural policies, in what have been largely local-authority-led bids for government funds.

From the point of view of rural practice, one of the significant features of the 1980s was a growth in short-term project work of two main sorts: local generic community work projects (sometimes called 'patch-work'); and specialist community-orientated work (based on a single subject like housing, public transport, parish councils or young children). In too many cases, the short length of time has been due to funding limitations rather than because two or three years has been felt to be an appropriate time to do this sort of work. Funding limitations have also pushed some agencies into employing part-time staff, which is a reasonable way of accommodating men and women responsible for young dependants, of recruiting indigenous workers who already have a part-time occupation, or of working a very small 'patch'. It can also be part of a positive move to draw-in specialist skills to a community project, or to enable a project to employ several workers, who can then provide mutual support. However, too often part-time work has meant cutting corners, skimping on the necessary management, support and training, and leaving little time to develop an effective form of practice. Regrettably, one of the most lasting legacies of the 1980s is likely to be the association between rural community work 'on the cheap', and insufficient attention to concerns about effective practice.

It is essential that community work practice is sensitive and appropriate to the needs and nature of its constituent communities. Therefore, if practice must adjust to changes in rural areas there has to be a concern by the community worker for strategy and vision.

Key factors

It would be foolish to try and predict the future state of the rural UK in any detail but we can identify key factors which may have a significant bearing on those aspects of rural areas and communities which are of interest to community workers.

Firstly, the costs of personal mobility will be crucial. The relative cheapness of car and rail travel in the late 1970s and 1980s has seen the extension of commuting and 'second home' distances around every city and town. However, as we saw both in the early 1970s and early 1990s when world oil prices increased significantly within a matter of weeks, rural areas are very vulnerable to travel costs. If these costs continue to be fairly cheap, we can expect a continuation of urban pressures on the countryside: relatively wealthy former urban dwellers living in villages, but keeping their links with towns and cities for their leisure, shopping and employment. Rural house prices will continue to rise, local rural people will be displaced, facilities which are used mainly by local people will close, and there will be hardship not only for the remaining rural working class, but also for those incomers who are not so well-off. The increased use of new communications technology, and the consequent reduction in some people's travel, will only partially offset these trends. Contrasts within rural communities, based on social class, wealth, differing values etc., will then be greater than ever, and those in greatest need may well retreat even further from community life into the isolation of their own households.

Closely linked to the price of personal mobility is the value placed by society on living in rural areas. Villages are increasingly popular places in which to live, especially so in England and Wales, but we can foresee similar pressures happening in Scotland and Northern Ireland. The middle-class cult of a house in the country, where 'nothing must change after I have moved in', seems likely to spread, with clear implications for the nature and composition of rural communities. It is difficult to foresee whether the increased interest in 'green issues' will reinforce this attitude, or promote a wider concern for 'balanced communities'.

We see no immediate reason why the trends towards the 'decline of community' will not continue: participation and active involvement in community affairs may become even more of a minority occupation, as more people retreat to a home-centred life, or one based on leisure activities outside the local area. At the same time, we may well see an increase in what has been called the 'new villagers', the rural re-settlers who are making a conscious decision to live, work and actively participate in a rural community. In many ways this is a continuation or progression from the 1970s back-to-the-land, good life movement, and community workers have found that these people can often make a positive contribution of ideas, talents and time to the community, and are concerned to do this in a sensitive way which is appropriate to the local culture (Rural Resettlement Group, 1984; ACRE, Suffolk, 1991).

Future government policies will also be of importance. Current trends in agricultural policy are pointing towards: less financial support for farmers; a concern for less environmentally threatening methods; a need for greater diversification, enterprise and alternative land use strategies; and a generally less protective attitude by government. Many farmers, especially in the upland and remoter areas, will not be in the relatively happy position which they knew in the 1960s and 1970s, with implications for the overall health of some local rural economies, as well as for agricultural employment levels. However, this belt-tightening exercise will not affect all farmers in the same way, and it may be that some of those who did well in the past will prosper in the future.

Arguably more important for a much larger section of the rural population will be the impact of government policies on the role of local government and public services. In contrast to much of the 1970s, the 1980s saw cutbacks in the power and resources of local authorities which had a disproportionately large impact on the rural areas, where the economics of service provision were more precarious. Closures of rural hospitals and schools, cutbacks in social services and council house building, and reductions in funding for local voluntary sector activities are all the products of an intentional policy to curtail local and central government expenditure. This, and reductions in state power to provide services, will have two major consequences for rural areas: the continued centralisation of services into the towns and key settlements, where they can be more competitive and 'efficient', and a greater reliance on community (and individual) based voluntary support and self-help to meet vital services such as social care.

Themes for the 1990s

The experience of rural community work, in its various guises, since the 1920s is that it has changed in a number of ways: the increased volume of activity carried out; the relative importance of the voluntary and statutory sectors; the shift in balance from area-wide policy work towards local work; the balance between long-term and project work; the significance of particular issues; the relationship to 'the state'.

However, one of the most surprising things is that rural community work in all of its history rarely seems to have been in charge of its own direction or destiny. It is as if there have been hundreds of focal points of rural community work throughout the UK, all doing their own thing, largely in isolation from each other, and with relatively little capacity to learn and improve this practice. For many agencies and projects, 'innovation' has been little more than implementing the latest fashionable community work tool that is nationally available: for example, the ACRE and 'Local Jigsaw' approaches to village appraisals, the ACRE and Rural Housing Trust approach to rural housing development, the Shropshire RCC village contact scheme, the Galway type of adult education initiative.

While it is entirely right that good ideas should be disseminated and then experimented with elsewhere, we feel that the above trends are symptomatic of a rural community work movement which is in need of a more strategic approach: one which makes sense of the needs and nature of the local situation, and which may or may not be in line with some national formula. However, lest this is seen as some kind of parochial individualism, we feel that this is best achieved through better collaboration, cross-national learning, dissemination of good-practice, and sharing of analytical and evaluative information. This concern is the basis for the key themes which we identify for rural community work in the 1990s.

(i) *Consolidating the community work occupation.* An astonishing number of people have been practising community work in rural areas without realising it, or at least without being able to put a name to it. We do not believe that a new and distinct profession needs to be created but there is some sense in fostering a community of interest among practitioners in the UK. The first step in this process must be to recognise the commonality among those involved with the development of people and groups. Then, it is important to accept that within this commonality there is diversity, rather than to draw tight boundaries. The idea would be to build upon the common interest between fieldworkers from different agencies, and resource-providers, policy-makers and other occupations which are taking a community focus to their work. The basis of this process would be to expose rural community workers to a much wider array of ideas, values and experience, from a variety of settings, but all of which would be of relevance to their practice.

An important objective would be to promote learning about practice across the UK. It is all too easy to be parochial and say 'I can't learn anything from the Scottish Highlands of benefit to my practice in Surrey', or 'I can't imagine anyone in nonconformist Wales wanting to know about my experiences in Catholic Armagh', but we have found a wealth of experience which deserves a wider and more diverse audience. For example, Northern Ireland has a considerable amount of practical material about working constructively with social conflict and cultural differences within communities, while community workers in (for example) Wales or Cornwall have been ill-equipped to address conflict in their constituencies. The details of the situations may be different, but many of the principles are the same. Another example is village hall development work, which Scottish Community Education workers are having to address with a relative absence of supportive information and expertise, while just about every English rural community council has decades of experience of this line of work, backed up by a specialist national resource centre. The wider recognition by rural practitioners that they were doing community work would also bridge the gap between rural and urban, and we are convinced that the rural world has a lot to learn from the extensive range of practical and theoretical material based on urban practice.

The point which we would emphasise is that rural community work must be underpinned by stronger theory. Our advocacy of a sense of 'common occupation' rests as much on the need for critical analysis and clarification of key ideas such as 'community', 'participation' and 'development', as it does on the benefits arising from opportunities to exchange practical experiences. This point is emphasised by Henry Buller and Sue Wright (1990) in their critique of the woolly thinking underlying much British rural development policy and practice, in which they point to the importance for rural community work in particular to adopt a wider, international perspective.

(ii) *Promoting a 'community' approach.* The consolidation of the rural community work occupation would provide a larger and more coherent voice to influence practice-related issues in the UK: for example, to make the case to the Welsh Development Agency and Highlands and Islands Enterprise to provide long-term resources for rural community work, or to help universities and colleges to develop a rural focus in their degree and diploma courses.

Critical issues which are likely to dominate the 1990s, and which lend themselves to making greater use of community work methods, are: the struggle for affordable rural housing; working out the tensions between conservation and development policies; the delivery of community care services; and the search for effective and responsive local government. The involvement of local people in conducting appraisals of housing need, and subsequently negotiating with housing associations and local authorities to make appropriate provision, points to a growing recognition of the community-based approach. Similarly, there is growing awareness of the role which community groups can play in the town and country planning arena (see, for example, the UK Government White Paper *Our Common Inheritance*, DOE, 1990), and in the organisation of a wide range of social care and welfare services. In the field of local government, it seems likely that the very local tier will assume a higher profile. As *Faith in the Countryside* has observed (ACORA, 1990):

> there is, especially by comparison with other European countries, a relatively poor tradition of vibrant parish government in England. However, the increase in rural population and in particular the change to an increasingly articulate, locally-concerned rural population might be seen as presaging a burgeoning of local democracy where, albeit within a wide national and even European structure, local village communities are encouraged to decide more for themselves.

If stronger parish-level government is to avoid the risk of being municipal bureaucracy on a smaller scale, it will be important to secure the basic principles of a participatory democracy, of a sense of equality and justice, and of enabling groups and individuals to determine their own priorities. These, and the other key issues of the 1990s, are surely a compelling argument for community work to move towards the centre stage.

(iii) *The European perspective.* For many practitioners whom we talked to in the UK, the EEC was a far-away institution which meddled in affairs such as food labelling or the imposition of value-added tax on village halls, and '1992' was something to do with businesses and therefore outside the interest of community work. In contrast, we found some rural community workers, notably in Ireland (North and South), who have a working knowledge of the EEC institutions and its structural funds, and have forged practice-exchange links with their opposite numbers in mainland European countries. We have little doubt that they are better placed to help rural communities take advantage of a more 'open Europe'.

We can only see the European dimension growing in the 1990s, and rural community workers (like many other people) must learn to swim, or they will sink. National networks of community groups have become accustomed to lobbying and negotiating with national governments; they must extend this to the European tier.

The European Commission's *Future of Rural Society* (1988) signals a determination by policy-makers to develop a comprehensive European rural policy. It is crucial that community workers put forward their experiences and ideas into this unfolding debate, which so far remains dominated by economic considerations. This is especially important given the political pressures to reduce the pre-eminence of agriculture within European policy, and evidence that the peripheral rural areas of Europe will suffer as a result of the Single European Market.

Involvement in international groupings, such as the European Anti-Poverty Network, which brings together voluntary and community groups in order to influence policies and share experiences, is one way of ensuring that there is a rural community work input. Indeed, the successful networking achieved by the thirteen Integrated Rural Action Projects of the Second EC Poverty Programme (1985–1989) provides a useful model in this respect. It suggests that, if community workers are to be alert to the social, economic and cultural impact of the 'new Europe' (regional imbalances, increase in unemployment, 'social dumping' by companies), they will need to be well-organised, and be increasingly sophisticated in their knowledge of European developments and networks. The potential of new technology for rural areas, chiefly through the setting-up of 'telecottages', is a clear example of this: it is a Europe-wide development, there are EC resources for it, and there is a need to ensure that telecottages have a social rather than only an individualist application (see ACRE/Centre for Rural Studies, 1990).

The European dimension of social policy will undoubtedly grow in the 1990s, and rural community workers must learn to engage with it. There will be opportunities as well as constraints, and to take advantage of them will require new attitudes of mind, to think on a wider scale, and to forge new links with rural community work bodies in other European states.

(iv) *A reappraisal of values.* The growth of rural community work over the last few decades has not been matched by a clearer understanding of 'what is it all for' and just what it should be achieving. If anything, efficiency drives have pushed aside a concern for values in favour of value for money.

There is a need to reappraise our concepts of 'rural' and 'community' in the light of the socially mixed communities which are becoming the norm in many parts of the UK. As the romantic notion of traditional rural communities becomes increasingly untenable as an object of preservation, let alone of development, we need to evolve new visions of what it is about the complex social systems in villages and other rural localities that we are trying to maintain, change or enhance.

At the same time, we need to reorientate our values and aims in relation to the balance or choice between functional and developmental purposes in community work. Through a complex range of reasons which are only partly attributable to the attitudes of funders, most rural community work has been preoccupied with functional purposes: getting village halls built, helping parish councils to fight school closures, organising a voluntary minibus. The outcome of these processes may well be new, or retained, facilities in the village, but it has not necessarily done much to make the community a more caring, alert, participative, mutually supportive or resourceful network of people. If we ignore these developmental aspects, and the processes involved, can we seriously expect a community group which has recently saved its local bus service to be any better equipped to address the next crisis, let alone the subtle needs and aspirations of the silent, non-joiners which are not so glaringly obvious? And can we really expect people to engage in a positive way in wider political systems affecting their localities if they have been fed on a restricted community work diet of self-help? A challenge of the 1990s is to rediscover the developmental values of rural community work, and to celebrate them, rather than apologise for them.

A reappraisal of our values must also take account of people's prejudices and fears. Rural communities are just as likely, or even more so, to exhibit racism, sexism, age-ism and all the other aspects of intolerance and prejudice, although some have not yet had much chance to show it. It seems unlikely that there will be a significant growth of the ethnic minority population in rural areas in the 1990s. However, travellers and gypsies are noticeably disadvantaged minorities in some rural areas, and rural community work practice is now only beginning to find ways of promoting mutual tolerance and respect (see, for example, Fay and Crowley, 1990).

Gender issues, focusing on the role and opportunities for women, will need to take a higher profile among rural community workers (see, for example, Rural Enterprise Unit, 1988). Many rural voluntary bodies have not been well equipped to address questions of equal opportunities (National Council for Voluntary Organisations, 1989).

It is important for wider community reasons that rural areas do not become the breeding grounds of prejudiced people 'escaping' from the cities, or even the bastions of indigenous intolerance. It is not only timely that these attitudes should be confronted. It will be of increasing significance if the government's 'care in the community' proposals bring about a marked increase in people with special needs (such as those who have a physical handicap or learning difficulty) moving to, or remaining in, villages as well as towns.

(v) *Responsibility and citizenship.* It is not sufficient for community-based action to get things done within and for the locality. Rural community work will have failed if it promotes a wholly parochial attitude whereby individual communities make demands and secure some resources, without regard for the wider world.

Following the self- and household-orientated 1980s, there are growing concerns for the need to change our political culture: to evolve the individual into the active, responsible citizen. The growth of the 'corporate state' and of powerful private corporations, needs to be challenged and balanced by concerned and caring citizens, and so should urban-dominated attitudes which dismiss rural values.

Community work has a key part to play in this process, which David Thomas (1983) has described as 'franchisal development'. The development of communal coherence and the acquisition of resources are not only ends in themselves, but also a means whereby 'ordinary people' develop the knowledge, skills, confidence and commitment to take part in the wider society and the state, beyond the confines of the local community.

Franchisal development involves the development of political significance (helping people to gain a sense of worth, to feel part of a wider system, and to feel valued) and of political competence (thinking more flexibly and imaginatively, gaining insight into local and wider issues, and developing the skills to tackle them).

The challenge for the community worker is to build an agenda for developing political responsibility and citizenship, and one which is appropriate to the local culture. In doing so, the community worker will not be alone. There is a growing interest and commitment to these concepts by the church (ACORA, 1990), by Parliament (Commission on Citizenship, 1990) and, we suspect, in a variety of other institutions.

(vi) *A concern for strategy and effectiveness.* The concept of 'a good person making themselves available for what the community wants' is not a firm basis for good community work practice. The fact that resources concerned with the development of people in most rural areas are scarce, and that most rural people are grateful for what they get given, is not a good reason for community work to be complacent about quality. A concern for matching the community work response to the needs and nature of the communities and to the resources available, should be the foremost concern of every community work agency.

Whether it is at the level of the whole agency, or of an individual community work activist operating within a single community, we believe that an attention to strategy is most important and will become increasingly so. It is at this level that partnership and lobbying of government agencies, notably the Rural Development Commission and the Countryside Commission, is crucial. A strategic approach is not only the basis of good practice 'on the ground': it is the only viable way of influencing hard-minded local and central government politicians, and other agencies, to support rural community work and take it seriously.

Therefore it is not only a question of whether rural communities will survive and flourish: we believe that rural community work practice itself must develop a stronger preoccupation with strategy, if it is to have a future.

This book lays out some of the methods, skills, knowledge values and issues which make up this good practice.

References

Abrams, P. (1980) 'Social Change, Social Networks and Neighbourhood Care', *Social Work Service*, no. 22, February, pp. 12–23.

ACRE (1988) *Rural Advice and Information*, Cirencester, ACRE.

ACRE (1989) *Taking Stock of Your Parish*, Cirencester, ACRE.

ACRE, Suffolk (1991) *The Integration of Newcomers*, Cirencester, ACRE.

ACRE/Centre for Rural Studies (1990) *Teleworking and Telecottages*, ACRE.

Alexander, K. (Chairman) (1975) *Adult Education: The Challenge of Change*, London, HMSO.

Almond, G. A. and Verba, S. (1963) *The Civic Culture: Political Attitudes and Democracy in Five Nations*, New Jersey, Princeton University Press.

Andrews, P. (1988) *Local Life*, Wirksworth, Derbyshire Rural Community Council.

Antur Waunfawr (undated), Bryn Pistyll, Waunfawr, Caenarfon, Gwynedd.

ACORA – Archbishops' Commission on Rural Areas (1990) *Faith in the Countryside*, Worthing, Churchman.

Archbishops' Commission on Urban Priority Areas (1985) *Faith in the City*, London, Church House.

Armstrong, H. and Thompson, C. (1986) *Community Care in Rural Areas*, London, NCVO.

Aves, G. M. (1969) *The Voluntary Worker in the Social Services*, London, George Allen & Unwin.

Bailey, T. and Scott, I. (1989) *Rural Arts – A Discussion Document for the Calouste Gulbenkian Foundation*, London, Gulbenkian.

Ball, M. (1988) *Evaluation in the Voluntary Sector*, London, Forbes Trust.

Banks, S. (1990) 'Adult Education and Rural Community Development', *Adults Learning*, vol. 1 no. 8.

Batten, T. R. (1967) *The Non-Directive Approach in Group and Community Work*, London, Oxford University Press.

Benfield, G. (1990) *Rural Deprivation and Community Work*, Swansea, School of Social Studies, University College of Swansea and CDF.

Benington, J. (1989) 'An Assessment of the Rural Action Project' in Rural Action Project (1989).

149

Berwickshire Girls Work Project (1988) *Berwickshire Girls*, Borders Regional Council.

Beveridge, Lord (1948) *Voluntary Action: A Report on Methods of Social Advance*, London, George Allen & Unwin.

Borders Regional Council, Community Education Service (1989) *Pilot Study in Staff Development and Career Review*, Galashiels, Borders Regional Council.

Brasnett, M. (1969) *Voluntary Social Action: A History of the National Council of Social Service*, London, NCSS.

British Broadcasting Corporation (1978) *The People's Activities and Use of Time: A Reference Book Based on 2 Surveys of Great Britain 1974–75*, London, BBC.

Brody, H. (1973) *Inishkillane. Change and Decline in the West of Ireland*, London, Faber & Faber.

Bryant, B. and Butcher, S. (undated) *Setting Up a Community Company in a Rural Area*, Association of Community Workers, Occasional Paper 1.

Buller, H. and Wright, S. (eds) (1990) *Rural Development: Problems and Practices*, Aldershot, Gower.

Butcher, H., Cole, I. and Glen, A. (1976) *Information and Action Services for Rural Areas*, York, University of York, Dept. of Social Administration and Social Work.

Butcher, H., Collis, P., Glen, A. and Sills, P. (1980) *Community Groups in Action: Case Studies and Analysis*, London, Routledge & Kegan Paul.

Cawkwell, T. (ed.) (1989) *A Talent for Caring – Community Care and Voluntary Action in Rural Norfolk*, Hingham, Norfolk Rural Community Council.

Champion, T. and Watkins, C. (eds) (1991) *People in the Countryside*, London, Chapman Publishing.

Cloke, P.J. (ed.) (1988) *Policies and Plans for Rural People*, London, Unwin Hyman.

Combat Poverty Agency (1990) *Community Work in Ireland*, Dublin, Combat Poverty Agency.

Commission on Citizenship (1990) *Encouraging Citizenship*, London, HMSO.

Commission of the European Communities (1988) *The Future of Rural Society*, COM(88), 371 final, Bulletin of the European Communities Supplement 4/88.

Community Council of Northumberland (1990) *Action with Communities in Northumberland*, Morpeth, Community Council of Northumberland.

Conlon, J. (1977) *Community Work in a Rural Health and Social Services District*, Belfast, Social Work Advisory Group, Dept. of Health and Social Services, Northern Ireland, no. 3.

Connor, A. (1977) *A Study of Six Parishes in North East Norfolk*, cited in Shaw (1978).

Corner, S. (1989) *Milton Community Profile*, Invergordon, Assoc. of Community Enterprises in the Highlands and Islands.

Deane, E. (ed.) (1990) *Lost Horizons, New Horizons: Community Development in Northern Ireland*, Belfast, WEA/Northern Ireland Community Development Review Group.

Department of the Environment (1990) *Our Common Inheritance*, London, HMSO.

Durham RCC (1990) *East Durham 2000*, Durham, Durham RCC.

European Commission (1988) *The Future of Rural Society*, Bulletin of the European Communities Supplement 4/88, Luxembourg, Office for Official Publication of the European Communities.

Fay, R. and Crowley, N. (1990) 'Travellers and Community Work', in *Community Work in Ireland*, Dublin, Combat Poverty Agency.

Feek, W. (1988) *Working Effectively: A Guide to Evaluation Techniques*, London, Bedford Square Press.

Feek, W. and Smith, D. (1984) *Value Judgements: Evaluating Community Based Work*, Leicester, National Youth Bureau.

Feuerstein, M. T. (1986) *Partners in Evaluation: Evaluating Development and Community Programmes*, London, Macmillan.

Fitzduff, M. (1990) 'Political Experiences and Community Development-Conflicting or Connecting?' in Deane (1990).

Fitzduff, N. (1992) 'Protest and Adult Education in Loughshore' in Henderson and Francis (1992).

Francis, D., Henderson, P. and Thomas, D.N. (1984) *A Survey of Community Workers in the United Kingdom*, London, NISW.

GRAIN (Gordon Rural Action and Information Network) (1989) *Seventh Annual Report*, Huntly, GRAIN.

Green, R. (1989) 'The Badenoch and Strathspey Social Work Team for the Highland Region' in *Pictures of Practice: Vol. 1. Community Social Work in Scotland*, eds G.G.Smale and W.Bennett, London, NISW.

Greeves, T. and Taylor, R (1987) *The Local Jigsaw: Village Appraisals and Parish Maps*, Countryside Commission and Development Commission.

Hedley, R. (1985) *Measuring Success: A Guide to Evaluation for Voluntary and Community Groups*, London, ADVANCE.

Henderson, P. and Francis, D. (eds) (1992) *Rural Action – A Collection of Community Work Case Studies*, London, Pluto Press in assoc. with ACRE/CDF.

Henderson, P. and Thomas, D.N. (1987) *Skills in Neighbourhood Work*, 2nd edn, London, Unwin Hyman.

Hereford and Worcester Rural Community Council (1981) *Wyeside Community Project 1978–80.*, Hereford, Hereford & Worcester RCC in conjunction with the County Council.

Institute of Welsh Affairs (1988) *Rural Wales: Population Changes and Current Attitudes*, Cardiff, Institute of Welsh Affairs.

Johnstone, W.D., Nicholson, C., Stone, M.K. and Taylor, R.E. (1990) *Countrywork*, Cirencester, ACRE/The Planning Exchange.

Justad, T. (1986) 'Building on Success', *Initiatives*, June.

Justad, T. (1990) 'Shetland: Mossbank & Firth Community Co-operative Ltd', in *Building Bridges into Work*, ed. McMichael, P., Lynch, B. and Wight, D., London, Longman.

Kennedy, S. and Kelleher, P. (1989) *Guidelines for Community Development Workers Second European Programme to Combat Poverty(1985–1989)*, Ireland, Focus Point Project Ltd.

Key, M., Hudson, P. and Armstrong, J. (1976) *Evaluation Theory and Community Work*, London, CPF.

Lewis, R and Talbot-Ponsonby, A. (eds) (1987) *The People, The Land and The Church,* Hereford, Hereford Diocesan Board of Finance.

Little, J. K. (1987) 'Gender Relations in Rural Areas: The Importance of Women's Domestic Role', *Journal of Rural Studies*, vol. 3, pp. 335–62.

Lowe, P., Bradley, T. and Wright, S. (eds) (1986) *Deprivation and Welfare in Rural Areas*, Norwich, Geobooks.

Lowe, P. and Buller, H. (1985) in Rogers, Blunden and Curry (1985), p. 64.

Lumb, R. (1989) *Infobus. A report on the Northumberland Rural Information Service*, Morpeth, Community Council of Northumberland.

Lumb, R. (1990) 'Rural Community Development; Process versus Product', in Buller and Wright (1990).

Martinez-Brawley, E. E. (1982) *Rural Social and Community Work in the U.S. and Britain*, Praeger Special Studies.

Martinez-Brawley, E. E. (1986) 'Community Oriented Social Work in a Rural and Remote Hebridean Patch', *International Social Work*, vol. 29, no. 4, pp. 349–72.

McCartney, C. (1990) 'Community Development – Working With or Against the Community?', in Deane (1990).

McLaughlin, B. (1985) *Deprivation in Rural Areas – Final Report to the Department of the Environment*, Essex, Chelmer Institute of Higher Education.

McLaughlin, B. (1986) 'Rural Policy in the 1980s: The Revival of the Rural Idyll', *Journal of Rural Studies*, vol. 2, no. 4, pp. 81–90.

McLaughlin, B. (1987) 'Rural Policy into the 1990s – Self Help or Self Deception', *Journal of Rural Studies*, vol. 3, pp. 361–4.

Meadows, A. (1985) 'Involved', unpublished study arising from an Arkleton fellowship.

Meadows, A. and Turkie, A. (1988) *How Are We Doing? An Introduction to Self-Evaluation for Voluntary Groups*, London, NCVO.

Morrison, I. (1989) *It's Not What You Do…A Model for Evaluating Process*, no publisher.

Moseley, M. (1985) *The Waveney Project. The Role of the Catalyst in Rural Community Development*, Norwich, University of East Anglia.

Moyle, R. (Chairman) (1975) *Report of a Joint Working Party on Community, Sporting and Recreational Provision by District Councils*, Northern Ireland, Department of Education.

National Council for Voluntary Organisations, Rural Unit (1989) *Equal Opportunities – A Starter Pack for Groups in Rural Areas*, London, NCVO.

Newby, H. (1977) *The Deferential Worker*, Harmondsworth, Penguin.

Newby, H. (1980) *Green and Pleasant Land?*, Harmondsworth, Penguin.

Newby, H. (1987) *Country Life. A Social History of Rural England*, London, Weidenfeld & Nicholson.

Oakley, P. (1988) 'Conceptual Problems of the Monitoring and Evaluation of Qualitative Objectives of Rural Development', *Community Development Journal* vol. 23, no. 1 (January).

O'Donohue, K. (1990) 'Rural Development and Community Work', in *Community Work in Ireland*, Dublin, Combat Poverty Agency.

OPCS (1983) *General Household Survey 1981*, London, HMSO.

Pahl, R. E. (1966) 'The Rural–Urban Continuum', *Sociologia Ruralis iv.*

Payne, S. and Townsend, P. (1990) *Avon Rural Health Project – An Evaluation*, Bristol, University of Bristol, Dept. of Social Policy and Social Planning.

Pennine Rural Development Area Strategy Committee, West Yorkshire (1988) *Rural Development Programme 1989–1992*, submission to the Rural Development Commission.

Redcliffe-Maud (1969) *Community Attitudes Survey – Research Studies 9 – Royal Commission on Local Government in England*, London, HMSO.

Rogers, A. W. (1987) 'Voluntarism, Self-Help and Rural Community Development: Some Current Approaches', *Journal of Rural Studies*, vol. 3, pp. 353–60.

Rogers, A., Blunden, J. and Curry, N. (eds) (1985) *The Countryside Handbook*, London, Croom Helm.

Ross, M. and Lappin, B. W. (1967) *Community Organization*, 2nd edn, New York, Harper & Row.

Rothman, J. (1969) 'An Analysis of Goals and Roles in Community Organisation Practice', in *Readings in Community Organisation Practice*, 1st edn, ed. Kramer, R. and Specht, H., Englewood Cliffs, NJ, Prentice-Hall.

Rothman, J. (1974) 'Three Models of Community Organisation Practice', in *Strategies of Community organisation*, 2nd edn, ed. F. M. Cox *et al.*, Itasca, Ill., Peacock.

Rural Action Project (1989), *Rural Development – A Challenge for the 1990s*, Londonderry, RAP, N.I.

Rural Enterprise Unit (1988) *Women in the Countryside*, Stoneleigh, Royal Agricultural Society of England.

Rural Resettlement Group (1984) *Rural Resettlement Handbook*, Prism Alpha in assoc. with Lightfoot Books.

Russell, A. J. (1986) *The Country Parish*, London, SPCK.

Scott, I., Denman, J. and Lane, B. (1989) *Doing by Learning*, Cirencester, ACRE.

Scott, D., Shenton, N. and Healey, B. (1991) *Hidden Deprivation in the Countryside*, Glossop, Peak Park Trust.

Self-Help Alliance (1988) *Self-help in Rural Areas – Is It Different?*, London, Tavistock Institute of Human Relations.

Shaw, J. M. (1978) 'Social Implications of Village Development', in M. J. Moseley (ed.), *Social Issues in Rural Norfolk*, Norwich, University of East Anglia.

Smith, W. P. and Bate, H. A. (1953) *Family Casework and the Country Dweller*, London, Family Welfare Association.

Spergel, I. A. (1969) *Community Problem Solving*, Chicago, University of Chicago Press.

Stacey, M. (1969) 'The Myth of Community Studies', *British Journal of Sociology*, vol. 20.

Standing Conference of Rural Community Councils (1986) *Rural Patchworkers' Training Conference – Summary Report*, London, SCRCC/CPF.

Taylor, H. (1976) *An Evaluation of the Effectiveness of Social Services Provision in a Rural Area*, Birmingham, Dept. of Soc. Admin., University of Birmingham.

Thomas, D. N. (1983) *The Making of Community Work*, London, George Allen & Unwin.

Thomas, D. N. and Warburton, W. (1977) *Community Workers in Social Services Departments: A Case Study*, London, NISW/Personal Social Services Council.

Townsend, P. (1979) *Poverty in the United Kingdom,* Harmondsworth, Penguin.

Twelvetrees, A. (1991) *Community Work*, 2nd edn, London, Macmillan.

Von Hoffman, N. (1972) 'Finding and Making Leaders', abstracted in *Community Organisers and Social Planners*, ed. J. L. Ecklein and A. A. Lauffer, New York, Wiley.

West Glamorgan Council for Voluntary Service (1990) *Valleys Project – Final Report*, Swansea, WGCVS.

Williams, G (1984) *Rural Self-Help: Institutional Instrument or Policy Objective in Rural Development?*, Gloucestershire Papers in Local and Rural Planning, Issue no. 23.

Williams, R. (1973) *The Country and the City*, London, The Hogarth Press.

Wright, S.(1990) 'Development Theory and Community Development Practice', in Buller and Wright (1990).

Young, C. (1990) *Planning for Rural Care*, London, NCVO.

Index